THE *Woman's*
Bowling GUIDE

THE *Woman's* Bowling GUIDE

BY SYLVIA WENE

DAVID McKAY COMPANY, INC.
NEW YORK

Wene, Sylvia.   The woman's bowling guide.   New York, D. McKay Co.
[1959]   113   p.   illus.   26   cm.   1.   Bowling.   i.   Title.   GV903.W44
794.6   59–9383 ‡   Library of Congress

To

OUR WOMEN BOWLERS

*In honor of the four important pins in
their lives: bobby, rolling, diaper—
and, now, the bowling pin.*

Contents

THE *Woman's*
Bowling GUIDE

Introduction

WHEN I WAS SEVENTEEN YEARS OF AGE—AND ONLY FOUR FEET, ELEVEN inches tall—my brother and sister took me on my first visit to a bowling establishment.

"You," my brother stated, "are too small to bowl. So you just sit here and keep score."

The game looked like great fun and I wanted to try my hand at it. But, as ordered, I sat there and tried to keep score while they bowled.

But the next day I went back to those lanes with my mother to see how I would do. I wasn't very successful. As a matter of fact, I didn't come anywhere near 100. Mother did and, I suppose, that piqued me somewhat.

Anyhow, I decided that I was going to roll 100. It took me quite a while. And, by that time, I had decided that I wouldn't quit until I had rolled 200.

Then, by the time I was able to accomplish the 200, I was so crazy about the game that I was not able to give it up.

Now I am still only four feet, eleven inches tall.

Yet I am rather proud of my record:

First woman to bowl a perfect 300 game in sanctioned East Coast play.

A 206 national recorded average for three straight seasons.

The world record of eleven 700 series in one year.

National individual match game champion of 1955.

"Woman Bowler of the Year" for 1955.

SYLVIA WENE. At home in her bowling trophy room.

I am making it a point to accent these achievements to illustrate to you that stature has little to do with making you a better-than-average bowler.

Consider that there are some 25 million bowlers—and the national average, for both men and women, is below 150.

There is one major reason for this pin-toppling deficiency: a scarcity of expert instructors to give individual instruction.

The result is that most bowlers start by simply walking out on the lane with a few words of advice from a friend and roll away. If they approach the friend's peak efficiency—as low as it may be—they are satisfied and thereafter stay in a low-scoring rut from force of copied habit.

I am not trying to tell you that championship bowling is easy. It takes long hours of hard work. But bowling well—which means scoring higher than the national average—isn't at all difficult if you master the basic principles.

And, believe me, it is just as easy to learn the correct basic principles as it is to adopt improper ones.

There we have the purpose of this book. Here, illustrated in sequence photographs which should answer any and all questions, I have outlined in detail the form and technique of the champions.

If you are a novice, it will pay you well to read closely and put correct techniques into practice from the very beginning, avoiding the traps that waylay most untutored beginners. If you have been bowling for years and have settled into a low-scoring rut, I am certain that you will quickly be able to discover where you have been getting off the highway to high scores.

I also have attempted to make this more than a mere bowling instruction book. You will find all you need to know—all there is to know—about bowling: how to bowl, how to form your own league, the etiquette of the lanes, equipment, awards to be won, and the history of women's bowling.

Yet there is even more than that.

This is a book for women by a woman.

So I have included a chapter on bowling fashions and, with the help of Revlon, a section on sports make-up which is complete right down to the care of the nails—always expendable items when it comes to bowling.

Then, too, there is a section on home exercises which was prepared with the expert assistance of Joan Javer, New York regional supervisor for the Vic Tanny gym system of training. These were designed to trim your figure as well as fatten your score.

I wish to thank these people for their invaluable assistance. At the same time I must express my gratitude to Ben Rose, whose expert instruction permitted me to escape most of the pitfalls that trap the beginner; Mrs. Jeannette Knepprath, president of the Women's International Bowling Congress; George Sullivan and Carl Johnson of American Machine and Foundry; Carol Christensen, who modeled the fashions so beautifully; and Emil Lence of the Manhattan Bowling Lanes.

Only through their unstinting co-operation was it possible to give you a book which will put you in tune for ten-pin success.

SYLVIA WENE

1 *How women's bowling started*

THERE IS NO DEFINITE RECORD AS TO WHEN WOMEN BEGAN TO BOWL IN the United States, but it can be said without contradiction that women's influence and interest, as well as the bid for women's patronage, lifted the sport out of a back-alley limbo.

Bowling establishments of a half century ago were called by the descriptive name of "alleys." On the whole they were dark, dimly lit, and unattractive. They were confined mostly to evil-smelling basements and they spawned cutthroat gambling.

Today they are recreational fairylands where your young daughters may bowl in a clean, spacious atmosphere of complete safety. Much of the credit for the success and cleanup of bowling should go to the Bowling Proprietors of America. It was they who realized the value of the woman bowler and gave her the bright, shining facilities for sport, and even supervised nurseries for the small fry, who can play happily while Mother bowls.

Some credit must go, too, to those pioneer women who first organized bowling among women at St. Louis, Missouri, in 1907. The men's first American Bowling Congress tournament had been held in Chicago in 1901, and many women had begun accompanying their husbands to the tournament each year.

When the A.B.C.'s annual event was held in St. Louis in 1907, the women held a tournament following the men's. This procedure was followed in Cincinnati and Pittsburgh the next two years but then was abandoned as, for some inexplicable reason, the women's interest waned and there weren't enough competitors.

In the ultra-modern pin palaces of today even supervised nurseries are available where the kiddies play while Mother bowls.

Bowling has existed, in one form or another, since the days of the old cities of Egypt. Objects much like today's bowling balls and pins have been unearthed in an Egyptian grave which archaeologists have determined to date at about 5200 B.C. Northern Italy saw bowling in the time of the Caesars; and in Germany, in the third and fourth centuries A.D., the degree of skill displayed in striking down pins with a ball was said to be proof of the bowler's love of God and the goodness of his life. Holland was the center of much ninepins activity, and skittles flourished in England from the fourteenth century on.

The historic fascination of this game has been such that legend has Sir Francis Drake waving away excited messengers who interrupted his bowling game to tell him that the Spanish Armada was approaching England's shores. He told them quite coolly that there remained sufficient time for him to complete (and win) his game before going out to vanquish the enemy.

America first saw bowling in the form of ninepins, which the Knickerbockers introduced in 1626. The game gained such a following that, in 1732, the parade ground in front of Battery Fort was converted into

a bowling green, and this is the same Bowling Green that is now pre-
served on New York's lower Broadway.

Unfortunately, by 1841, the extremely popular sport of ninepins had
fallen under the control of organized gambling to such an extent that
the game itself was outlawed by the Connecticut state legislature. To
play the traditional game of ninepins became a crime punishable by a
fine. However, it proved impossible for those who had fallen under the
spell of the game to cease to bowl entirely, and so ninepins had a tenth
pin added, which changed the original triangular formation of the pins,
and altered the rules until the game became the one played today.

Two attempts at national organization for men failed before the
successful formation on September 9, 1895, of the current American
Bowling Congress, to which I am indebted for all historical information in this chapter. This group formulated our present rules, regula-
tions, and equipment specifications.

Women's interest in a national organization collapsed after the 1909
tournament in Pittsburgh, as mentioned earlier, and for six years there
was no competition.

THE WOMEN'S INTERNATIONAL BOWLING CONGRESS   Finally, when the
men held their tournament at St. Louis in 1916, the women decided
once again to attempt to form a national organization. This time it
became a reality, and the Women's International Bowling Congress
came into existence as a permanent organization. It started with 40
members. In 1958 its membership had risen to 1,005,000, when its ever
more successful annual tournament attracted 2,587 teams.

MEMBERSHIP   You can become a member by joining a sanctioned
league, but the W.I.B.C. has individual membership with which each
member receives her own membership card. The cost is $1.25 per
person per year, of which the W.I.B.C. receives fifty cents, the city
organization receives fifty cents, and the state organization receives
twenty-five cents.

ANNUAL TOURNAMENT   The annual W.I.B.C. tournament is a gala
affair with three divisions: teams with an average of 751 and over;

teams with an average of 651 to 750; and teams with an average of 650 or less.

Those who enter must use their highest average as of December 1 of the ensuing tournament year. All averages must be verified and the entry blank signed by the league secretary and the city association secretary.

The team bowling the highest total pins in the team event, regardless of the division in which it is entered, wins the W.I.B.C. championship.

To be eligible, a bowler must have bowled at least three games in a sanctioned league before December 1 of the ensuing tournament year. The entry closes two weeks or more before the date set for the opening.

Events consist of a five-woman-team contest, a two-woman-team contest, and an individual contest. The bowler with the largest total pins in the three events is the All-Events Champion.

Bowlers entered in the doubles also must compete in the singles, and the singles entrants also must compete in the doubles. The entry fee is $3 for each event.

Two days are required to bowl the nine games for those in all events. The team bowls on one day, and those entered in the singles and doubles bowl in those events the next day. All entrants are notified of the time they are scheduled to bowl at least three days before the tournament opens and the entrants must be on hand thirty minutes before they are scheduled to bowl.

The tournament rules provide that each five-woman team must have at least three balls to use and each two-woman team must have at least one ball.

AWARDS   The proficient woman bowler can win many awards.

If you roll a perfect 300 game, and if you are a member, the W.I.B.C. will present you with a gold ring. It also awards a silver ring for a 298 or 299 game, as well as medals for all games of 275 or better.

Several dress and blouse concerns which advertise in the *Woman Bowler* magazine award a $1,000 United States savings bond if you bowl a 300 game while wearing their products. If you manage this feat against A.M.F. pins, this company will make you a pair of book ends out of one of the pins and also present you with a gold wrist watch.

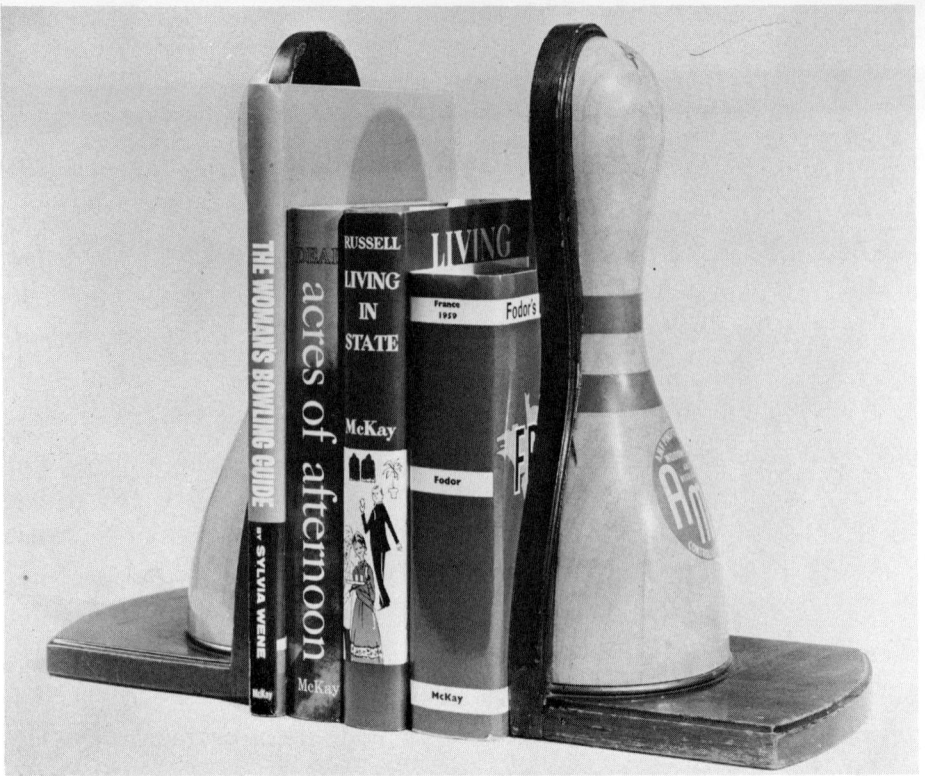

Many awards are available. Here are A.M.F. book ends, made out of the very pins against which you roll a 300 game.

Woman Bowler MAGAZINE   This is the official publication of the W.I.B.C. and can be obtained, ten issues per year, for $1.50

The magazine awards special arm emblems to subscribing W.I.B.C. members. These are for the "Dutch 200," a 200 game of alternate strikes and spares or vice versa; an all-spare game; a triplicate in which three game scores are identical; and conversion of the 7-10 and 4-6-7-10 splits.

T.V. BOWLING   Indicative of the increasing interest in women's bowling, the first major television network bowling show featuring women was presented in 1958-59.

Some of the nation's top women bowlers appeared, with the winner meeting a new opponent each week. The prizes included $600 to the winner each week and $200 to the loser, as well as $10,000 for a perfect 300 game. The woman rolling the highest third game for the entire show was to receive a mink coat, and the second highest third game a mink stole.

What you'll need to bowl 2

FIRST OF ALL I WOULD LIKE TO SUGGEST THAT YOU WILL DO YOUR BEST at bowling if you own your own equipment. You can manage by renting shoes at almost any establishment and using the "house balls," which are free.

But there is no substitute for your own bowling shoes, which fit comfortably and feel fitted to your feet. And if you have your own ball, you won't have to worry about finding a ball which fits your hand and which will work in the same manner all the time.

However, you may not wish to purchase your own ball until you decide whether you are going to bowl frequently enough to make it financially advisable. If this is the case, in the accompanying photos I am demonstrating how to get a comfortable and workable fit for your hand.

The first thing you should do, when selecting from among the house balls, is to place your thumb all the way into the thumb hole. Then, as I am demonstrating, place your two middle fingers over the finger holes so that the knuckles of your two middle fingers are directly over the finger holes. The crease underneath the knuckles should just clear the edge of the hole. Once you have taken your grip, there should be just enough space between your palm and the ball to insert a pencil.

In the group equipment picture you will see four types of bags, three types of balls, and the regulation bowling oxfords.

The ball bag and shoes on the left are a color innovation just brought out by A.M.F. This is a matching set with the shoes, bag, and even

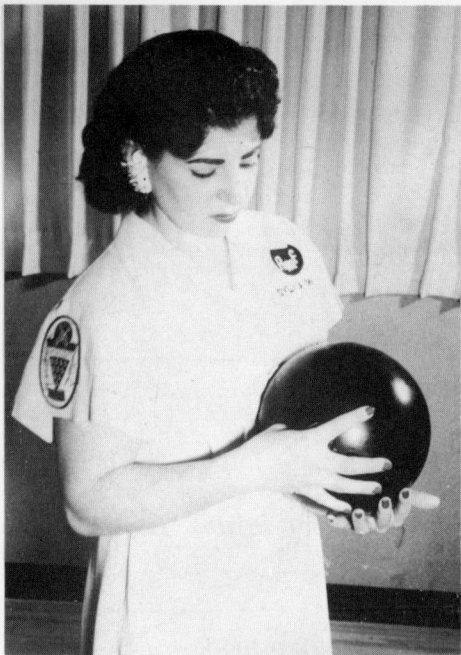

Left. Getting a fit with a house ball. The knuckles are over the finger holes with the underneath creases just past the rim of the holes. *Right*. There should be just enough space between palm and ball to insert an ordinary pencil.

the ball available in julep green or sea blue. The three-piece set costs $48.45, or the items may be purchased separately in either color, the ball for $31.75, the bag for $8.75, and the shoes for $7.95.

In the center is my "pro type" bag, too large for ordinary purposes. Beside it is a small shoe bag and on the right side is a man's bag of hand-tooled saddle leather which retails for $37.50. In front of it is a mottled ball with the ordinary black ball in the center.

THE BALL   Besides the familiar black, balls now come in pastel colors and mottled designs. Black models retail for about $25 and the mottled balls cost about $4 more. Even if you choose a lightweight ball, which means it has cork in the center, the cost is the same as for a regulation sixteen-pound ball.

Although it is possible to purchase stock balls with pre-drilled holes, a custom-drilled ball will provide a true fit. And fitting and drilling are free when you purchase your ball at a bowling pro shop.

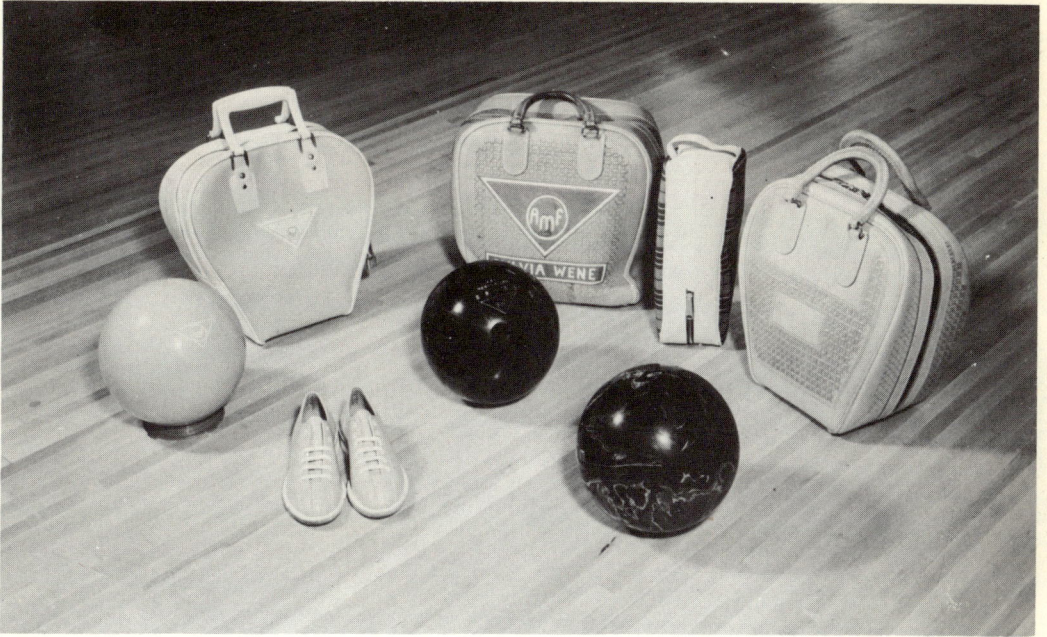

Various types of bags and balls described in detail in the text.

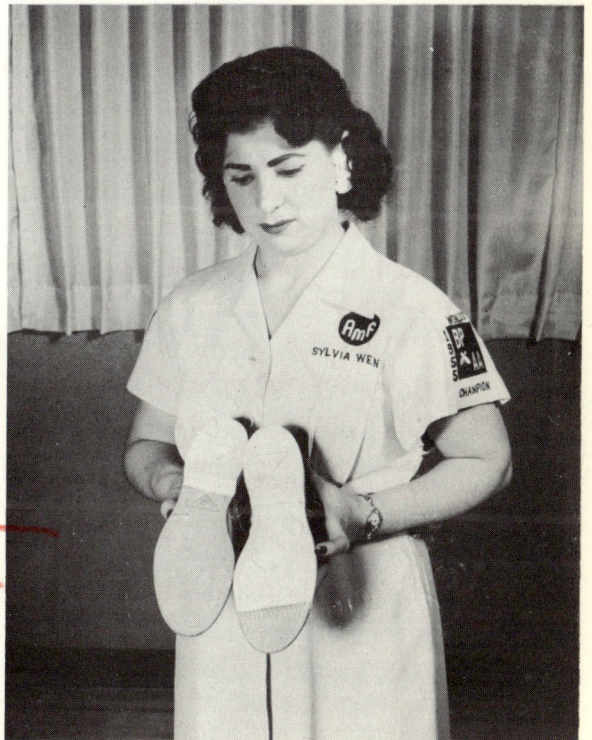

The bowling oxfords, with a sliding sole on the left shoe and a breaking sole on the right. This is reversed for left-handers.

Left. The thumb guard prevents soreness and blisters. *Center.* One type of wrist supporter. *Right.* The Pow-r-wrister prevents you from "breaking" your wrist.

BAGS   The small bag, designed to carry your shoes only, retails for about $2.50. Even the casual bowler should have his own shoes and one of these inexpensive cases in which to carry them. The larger bags for carrying both ball and shoes run anywhere from $6 to $30, although there are special models which range as high as $45.

SHOES   Bowling shoes have a sliding sole and special toe on the left foot and a braking sole on the right foot. If you are left-handed, remember that the sliding sole should be on the right shoe and the braking sole on the left foot.

There are many types of leathers and lasts and the general price range is from $5 to $16. You should not have to pay any more for the left-handed models. The shoes I am displaying in the accompanying photo are fine shoes which sell for approximately $8.

NEW ITEMS   One of the newest innovations in bowling accessories is the thumb guard which prevents soreness and blistering. This is par-

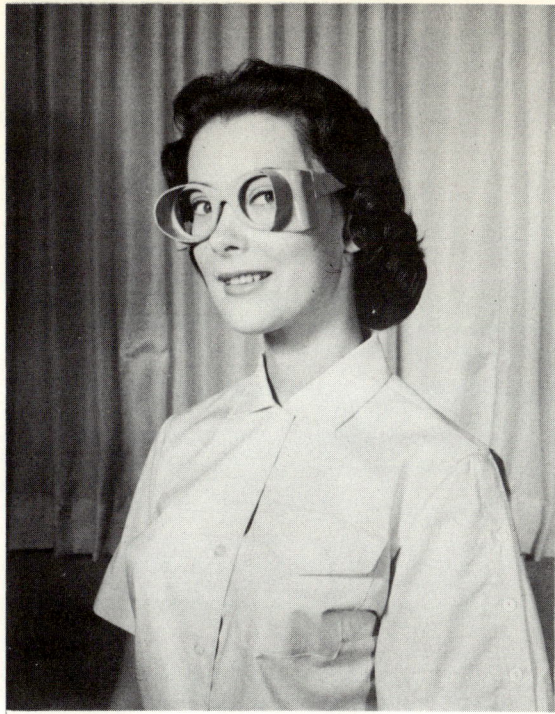

The Spiezio bowling blinders shut off distracting movements on adjoining lanes.

ticularly useful if you are going to do an excessive amount of bowling or if your thumb is particularly tender. Ben Rose, my instructor and manager, suggests that if you use one and find that the ball is slipping you might try cutting off the tip of the thumb glove. In this manner the thumb is still protected and the ball of the thumb is still free to give you a "feel" of the ball.

A wrist supporter can be helpful if you find that your wrist is tiring too much or you are "breaking" your wrist and are losing control of the ball.

Two different types are shown in the pictures. The first is an ordinary wrap-around support. The other is a leather guard designed to keep the hand and wrist in a straight line. This item, called the Pow-R-Wrister, straps around the wrist and over the back of the hand.

Here we have a picture of Carol Christensen modeling the Spiezio Bowling Blinders. These are put out for the bowler who is distracted by the movement of others on adjoining lanes. The blinders shut off this source of peripheral annoyance.

3 *What to wear*

With the ever-increasing number of women bowlers, fashion designers are creating new styles in a variety of modes and eye-appealing colors from which you can choose an outfit suited to your individual taste.

The majority of these outfits are designed with the dual purpose in mind of providing casual everyday wear as well as stylish and comfortable bowling costumes.

Generally speaking, blouse, skirts, and even one-piece dresses, are fashioned with pleats and flares which provide freedom of movement.

Too many women attempt to bowl in tight, binding skirts which prevent them from striding properly. Or they wear blouses which restrain their arm movement.

These specially designed bowling and casual-wear clothes are available at moderate prices. One-piece dresses with flared or pleated skirts, which are comfortable and easy to play in, sell in most stores for $7 to $15.

I prefer the one-piece gabardine dress which I am wearing in the accompanying photo. There are many styles of dresses, skirts, and blouses that come in a variety of colors and are manufactured at moderate prices by the Sport Queen Manufacturing Company of Detroit.

Carol Christensen is modeling another type of one-piece dress with a pleated back, flared skirt, and wide sleeve featured in most one-piece outfits. This one is two-toned gabardine with zipper front, retailing for $7.

My favorite
one-piece
gabardine dress
with the
wide skirt.

Another type
of one-piece dress
with pleated back
and zipper front.

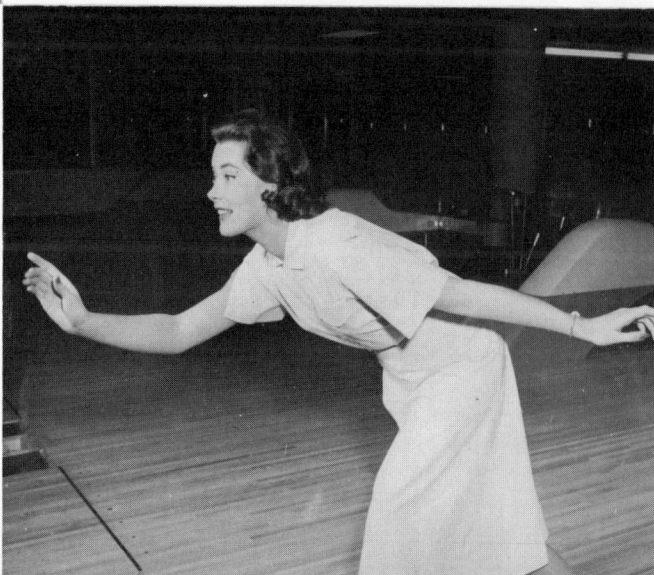

A blouse
with pleated back
and sleeves
which unbutton
to the shoulder
for greater arm
freedom.

Left. A knit-type T-shirt of great elasticity. *Center.* Zipped down, the Slaxkirt is a skirt. *Right.* Zipped up, it is a short slack permitting great freedom of movement.

A broadcloth skirt with a flap-over pleat in the back.

BLOUSES   In one photo, Carol is modeling a Macshore dual-purpose bowling blouse of drip-dry broadcloth, which comes in white, pink, blue, maize, beige, and green. Pleated to eliminate shoulder-blade bind, it has sleeves which unbutton up to the shoulder for further freedom. The shirt tail may be worn in or out. These blouses run the full gamut of even sizes, all the way up to 46. The tab on the pocket is perfect for the lettering of the team name. This blouse retails for $3.95. Similar blouses are available in prices ranging up to $6.

The other blouse Carol is modeling is a Ship 'n Shore knit T-shirt type. The elasticity of the knit fabric allows a great amount of freedom.

SKIRTS   One of the newest and particularly practical skirts is the Slax-kirt, a short slack and skirt all in one which sells for $10.95. As modeled here by Carol, it has a concealed zipper hidden under the front fly of the skirt. Zipped up it's a short slack; zipped down it's a dress skirt. Manufactured in seven colors, it comes in a wrinkle-resistant gabardine.

Also available are culotte-type skirts of rayon gabardine in the $5 to $7 price range which are extremely comfortable and practical.

Plain skirts come in a variety of styles and materials, featuring hidden pleats. One such, also modeled here by Carol, is the broadcloth skirt with the flap-over pleat in the back.

If you like to sew, any of the various pattern companies have designs for similar garments. These may be obtained at your local variety shops or department stores.

4 *In the beginning*

RHYTHM AND TIMING ARE THE TWO GREATEST ASSETS THAT WOMEN HAVE when it comes to bowling.

It is true that men have more strength. But women are naturally more graceful, and grace is rhythm and timing in motion.

However, the novice woman bowler, in the main, is afraid to let herself go. She holds her body stiff and refuses to "swing it."

Therefore, before we go into any of the basic principles, convince yourself that you aren't going to "look silly" if you keep your body loose and flexible when you do step up on the lane. Remember, nobody ever started as an expert. Eliminate the thought that you may look foolish— because if you give your natural rhythm and timing a chance to come through you have won half the battle.

BASIC PRINCIPLES Bowling is not a complex sport. You stand at the head of the lane; take three, four, or five steps as you choose; and roll the ball toward the waiting pins.

That's all there is to it.

Yet how you stand, how you take your steps, and how you release the ball spell the difference between success and failure.

Still, as I have said, it is not terribly complex. Actually it is rather simple.

If you absorb the basic principles.

If you were to come to me and ask me to teach you to bowl, I would show you first how to pick up the ball so that you wouldn't damage your

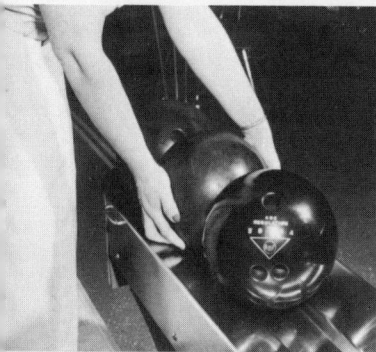

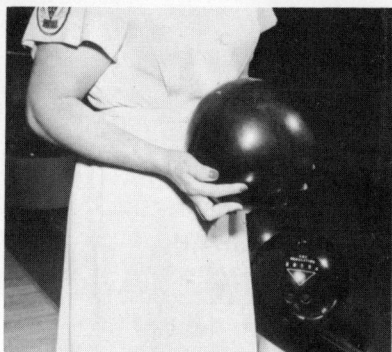

Left. Raise the ball with hands parallel to the rack. *Center.* Lift it to waist level with both hands. *Right.* Support the ball with the left hand while inserting the fingers.

arm and right there end your bowling career before it has even begun. Then I would teach you the stance and the seemingly intricate but actually easy footwork of the delivery.

Only when you had perfected those phases of bowling would I advance you to the business of perfecting one of the four different types of balls, using my system of shooting for spares, or learning how to play the various types of alleys.

As I said, first things first.

PICKING UP THE BALL   Fingernails are fragile items, and so are fingers. You can lose one, or both, or at least damage both painfully, if you aren't careful at the ball rack.

I am demonstrating in the photographs how you should pick up the ball.

First of all, always be certain that your hands are parallel to the line of balls. If you put your hands between the balls—see the accompanying photo showing how not to do it—a returning ball may roll against your hands or drive into another ball and smash it against your hands.

Observe that I raise the ball with both hands. Do not pick up the ball by merely inserting your fingers into the finger holes and hoisting. If you do, you give added strain to your wrist, fingers, and arms.

OWN YOUR OWN BALL   Establishments provide house balls free of charge, as I have noted, but you will find a tendency to want to use the same ball which you have picked out as your own special pet. If you are strong-willed enough, you may be able to talk the house out of the ball you consider "yours." But remember, it isn't. Thus, if you have to

settle for another, the minute difference in the boring of the hand span
—even though it may feel the same—will give you a different "work" on
the ball, or make it hook differently.

That's why I suggest that you buy your own ball if you are going to
be doing any considerable amount of bowling. Even for a once-a-week
league meeting you will find that your scores will be much higher in
the long run if you own a ball drilled to the exact dimensions of your
hand.

If you wish, you may start with a 10- or 12-pound three-fingered ball.
However, for regular use and maximum efficiency in getting the most
pins, you should not use a ball of less than 13 pounds. And if you have
the strength to handle it, I suggest a 15-pound ball.

An exceptionally light ball is fine for use while you are perfecting
your footwork. But I wouldn't advise buying a ball of less than 13
pounds because it simply won't carry the pins. Still, bear in mind that
if you attempt to use a ball that is too heavy it will ruin your rhythm
and thereby do more harm than a ball that for all practical purposes is
too light.

PRACTICE WITH ANOTHER BOWLER   As you begin to bowl, or even if you
are in a low-scoring rut, you probably will be or are making mistakes.

It is a good idea to get someone else to practice with. If possible, do
your bowling in the presence of a more experienced or better-than-

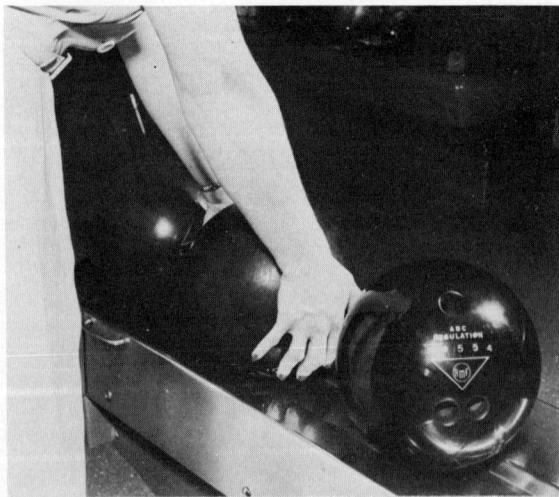

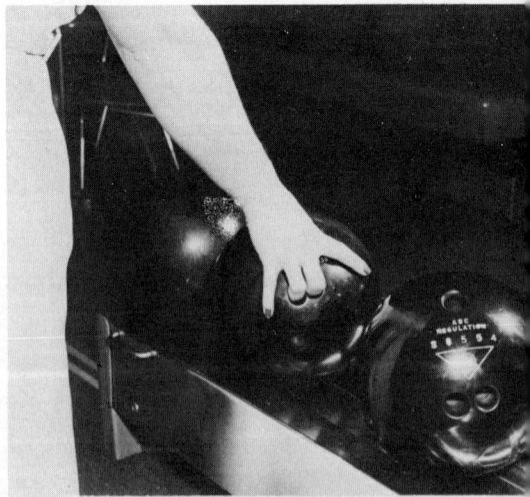

Left. Don't do it this way or you may pay with pinched or crushed fingers. *Right.* Nor
this way. You could injure your wrist or arm.

average bowler or a certified instructor. Then your partner can correct any faults you may have and can check the details of your game: whether you are taking your steps rhythmically, getting the proper elevation on your backswing, sliding with your shoulders squared to the pins, releasing the ball out in front of you and over the foul line, and whether you are following through properly.

BOWLING LEFT-HANDED   Regulation bowling shoes have a sliding sole on the left shoe and a rubber braking sole on the right shoe. This is reversed for the left-handed bowler—along with just about everything else.

The right-handed bowler starts the four-step delivery—the one I recommend—with the right foot. Naturally, the left-hander steps off first with the left foot.

Whereas the right-hander bowls for the 1-3 pocket from the right side of the lane, the left-hander starts from the left side of the lane and shoots for the 1-2 pocket.

However, the angles in shooting for spares, explained in a later chapter, are the same for the left-hander as for the right-handed bowler. The left-hander must line the left shoulder up, whereas the right-hander lines the right shoulder up with his target.

MOST COMMON ERRORS   Women bowlers on the whole make five major mistakes. These are: too slow an approach, too short a backswing, dropping the ball, a poor slide, and failure to follow through.

You must have enough speed to make a full, deep-kneed slide. This also will help you to get the ball out in front of you as you release it over the foul line.

For a strong, speedy delivery, begin your approach with a long push-away which will help you to swing the ball higher on the backswing and give your delivery the necessary momentum. That first movement of pushing the ball out away from your body helps pack power into your delivery.

Reviewing this advisory information which comes as a prelude to the actual business of bowling, keep in mind above all else that this is a sport whose very foundations are rhythm and timing—and master the basic principles before you start worrying about your scores.

5 *My favorite starting position*

THE SECRET OF BOWLING IS BALANCE. THIS MEANS BEING IN CONTROL OF your body from the moment you take your starting stance until you have completed your follow-through. If you lose your balance, you necessarily must lose control of the ball.

In my travels around the country, holding clinics and giving exhibitions, I have seen some extremely ludicrous starting positions. There are those who hold the ball so high that they almost have to stand on tiptoes to look over it. Others stoop over so far that the ball is almost touching the approach; and there are those who simply dangle the ball at their side.

It stands to reason that these bowlers are off balance before they begin the process of delivering the ball. Their rhythm and timing are shot to start with, because they must get into motion with a distinct lunge.

The result is a staggering approach to the foul line.

You can see, therefore, that a starting position in which you are properly balanced is of utmost importance.

The accompanying pictures show two acceptable stances. The first one is my favorite starting position.

In this position I have my left foot slightly in front of the right one, with my weight distributed evenly on both feet and the body comfortably erect. I am supporting the weight of the ball on the palm of my left hand with the ball held slightly above waist level.

Right here I would like to point out that the ball is held in the center of the body.

However, if you have extremely wide hips, you should hold the ball more to your right. This will enable you to clear your body more easily on the backswing. Meanwhile, if you'd like to do something at home about those hips, try the "hip roll" routine described and pictured in the chapter on exercises. (See p. 91.)

Ease and comfort are key requisites when you take your starting stance. And, because of the weight of the ball, you may feel you are better balanced when you use a slight crouch such as you can see in the accompanying photograph. This stance is acceptable from the standpoint of body balance but, as I pointed out, I prefer the more upright position or a slight crouch.

When taking your starting position, the height at which you hold the ball is of extreme importance. I would recommend that the ball never be held lower than the waistline or higher than the chin. These two positions are depicted in the photographs.

YOUR STARTING SPOT   As you will learn in the following chapter, there are three different approaches—the three-step, four-step, and five-step approaches—in the actual delivery of the ball. Naturally the point from which you start, known to bowlers as your "starting spot," will vary

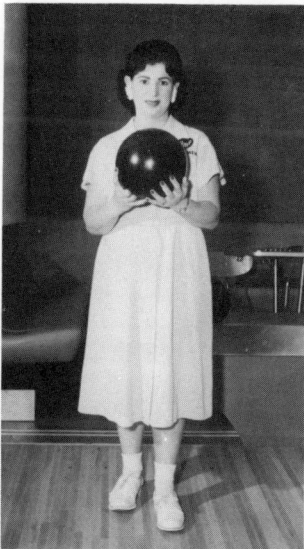

Front view
of the stance
I recommend.

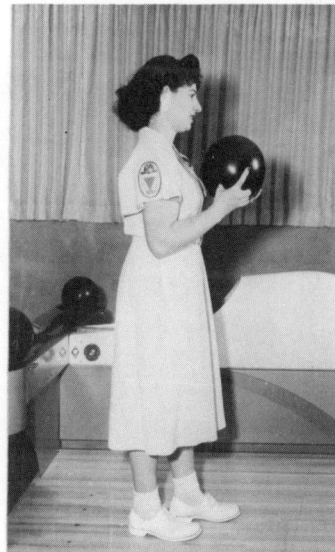

The stance
I prefer
seen from the
side.

according to the number of steps in your approach and the size of those steps.

I have found that it is fairly easy to locate this "spot" if you will simply go to the foul line, face away from the pins, and then pace off your steps. If you use a three-step delivery, pace back three and one-half steps, fixing in your mind at that distance a "spot" on the approach from which you will begin your delivery. Use this same procedure for the four-step and five-step deliveries. For the four-step delivery, pace off four and one-half easy steps from the foul line. For the five-step delivery, pace off five and one-half easy steps.

You will be able to make adjustments easily after rolling your first ball. If your slide has left you too far from the foul line, simply select a "starting spot" a bit closer to the foul line. If your slide is too close or over the foul line, move your "starting spot" back a similar distance.

Remember, though, if your "starting spot" is causing you to end up too far from the foul line, you probably will unconsciously try to compensate by taking strides which are too long and thereby throw yourself off balance. And if your "starting spot" is too close and you don't adjust, you will start taking shorter steps and won't get the full rhythm of your body into your delivery.

Finding this starting "spot" is extremely important. Many bowlers are too casual about finding a precise "spot" from which to begin their

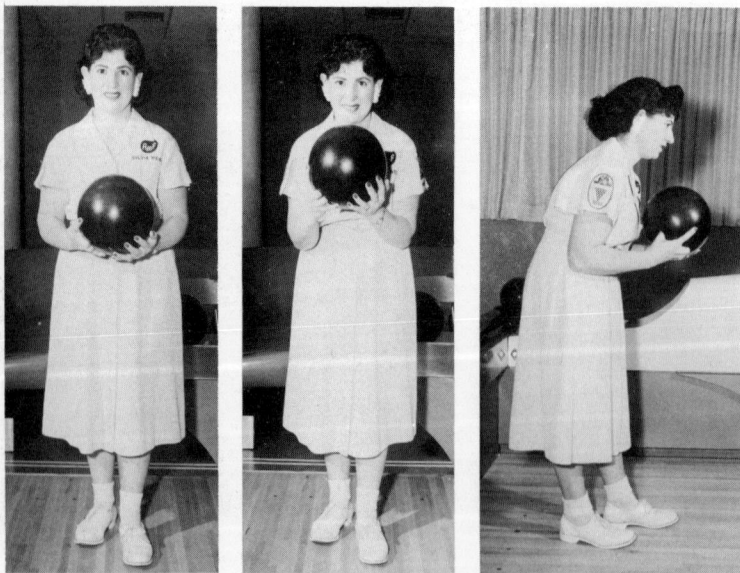

Left. The ball should be held no lower than this. *Center.* Nor higher than this. *Right.* This is the deepest crouch advisable.

delivery. Thus they make a strike, go back to a different starting position, throw the same ball, and wonder why they don't make another strike.

Every ball will vary if you change your starting position—which is why we change angles on the spare as detailed fully later. To prevent this variation on your "strike" ball, find the starting point that is best for you and use it every time.

Before summing up, let me add that comfort in your stance is vitally important. You can use either the erect or the slight-crouch position with the feet even or with the left foot slightly in front of the right one. But if you use the crouch, don't bend the head too far down. It is a rather common fault with women that when they use the head-down crouch they keep the head too far down even on the release and follow-through.

In recapping the starting position which I favor, remember that the weight of the body is distributed equally on both feet, or more weight on the right foot, and the shoulders are square to the pins. Keep the ball as close to the middle of the body as possible with the weight of the ball resting on the left palm, unless you have a hip problem or prefer to hold the ball slightly to the right side of the body.

This is the position I favor and I find that, while I am relaxed, my body seems to be in perfect balance for the start of the approach.

Below. Crouching this low, you can't possibly get started smoothly or receive the benefits of a pushaway. *Center.* You'd be surprised how many women take this kind of impossible stance. *Right.* You have to be off balance with this one, too.

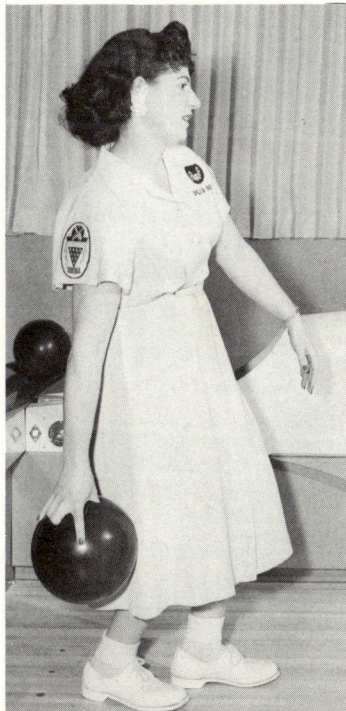

6 *My preferred four-step approach*

As we have noted before, there are three methods of actually delivering the ball.

Personally, I have always used, and suggest to my pupils, the four-step delivery. In this delivery you take your first step with the right foot, the second with the left, the third with the right, and then deliver the ball as you slide on the left foot in the fourth step-and-slide.

There also are three-step and five-step deliveries. In the three-step delivery you lead off on your left foot, take the second step with your right, and then step-and-slide on your left. In the five-step delivery you are merely getting the body into motion with a very short step off on the left foot and continue with the right foot on the second step as you would for a four-step delivery.

Bowling instructors have varied feelings as to which is the best approach for the novice. In almost every instance I do not hold with those who contend that a beginner should start with the three-step, because it requires less synchronization, and later shift to the smoother four- or five-step deliveries, for I feel that, particularly in the case of women, the three-step delivery puts too great a strain on the arm. However, once a certain approach has been learned it is not too difficult to shift to another.

But I would suggest that, even if at first it may be a bit harder to synchronize arm and foot action, you will be much better off in the long run if you start and stick to the four-step delivery which I have found so satisfactory.

THE PUSHAWAY   Regardless of which delivery you choose, the initiating factor of the entire approach is the pushaway.

There is nothing complicated about the pushaway. It is a simple movement which gets the body into motion naturally and smoothly.

You simply push the ball away from your body in a slightly downward path. Actually the weight of the ball pulls your body into motion.

If you aren't getting enough backswing and your ball lacks speed, a longer pushaway will take care of the deficiency. If you are getting too high a backswing and too much speed, simply cut down on the pushaway.

THE THREE-STEP APPROACH   In the accompanying sequence action photos you will see the hurried, rushing appearance I referred to earlier

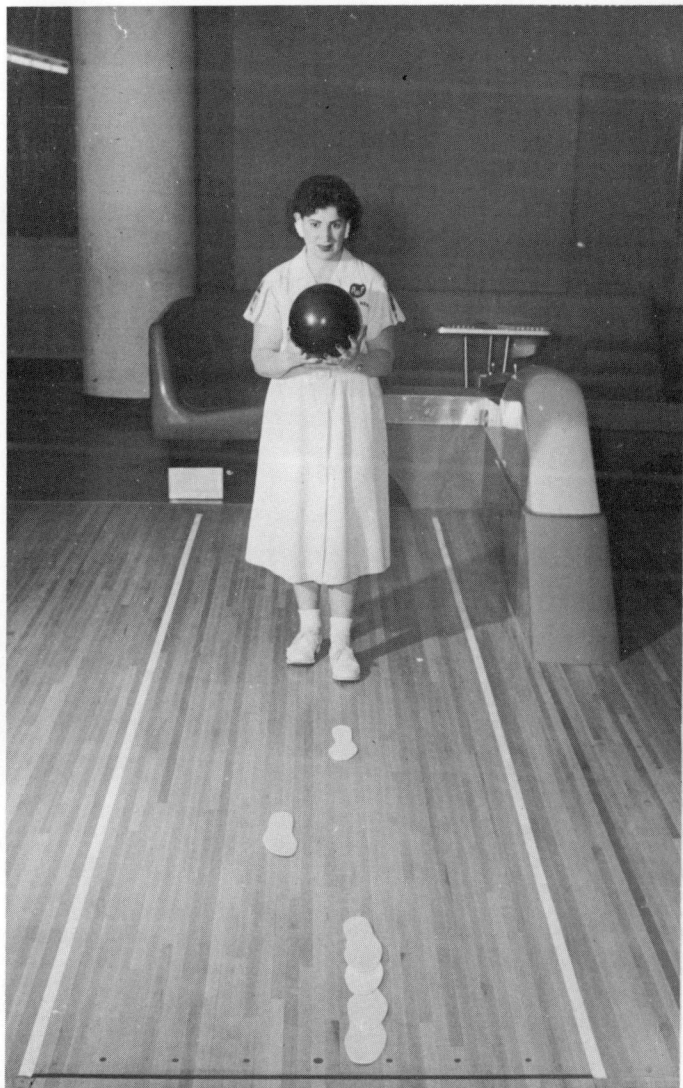

Foot patterns of the three-step approach.

Front view of the three-step approach, emphasizing the hurried action and body strain.

when I suggested that you by-pass the three-step delivery. This is because the entire delivery must be compressed into three steps.

Notice the hurried action of the arm, which the three-step delivery brings about. You will observe that before the first step is finished the ball is already well into the downswing. The body lunges into an extremely long first step which tends to throw it off balance.

As the second step is completed, the ball must already be at the top of the backswing. Now comes the third and final step. Only the strength of the arm pulls the ball through as you are making your slide.

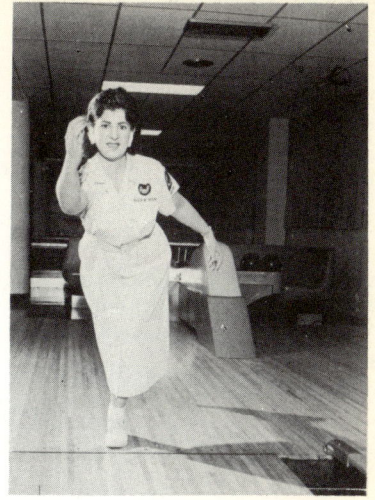

There are some highly successful three-step bowlers. But they must be strong and have exceptional balance to counteract the weight of the ball through the slide. It requires extra strength and balance to make a bent-kneed slide, keeping the shoulders squared to the pins, while the ball is being brought from behind the body.

One of the added perils of the three-step delivery is that, because of the extra strain on the body, the approach will be made in a zigzag fashion that will ruin your aim. If you use this approach, you must strive to keep your steps in a straight line.

Side view of the three-step delivery, again illustrating the difficulty of obtaining rhythm and timing.

THE FOUR-STEP APPROACH This is the delivery that I recommend strongly and I would like to caution you right here not to drive forward as if you were going to a fire. Rather than try for speed, you should attempt to become as methodical as a machine. A medium speed is best.

Learning to slow down was one of the hardest lessons I had to absorb. It wasn't until I stopped throwing a smoke ball that my scores began to go up.

The first step is the most important one in the four-step delivery, and if you start right you can finish right. Thus the right arm, the right foot, and the shoulders start forward as one on the pushaway.

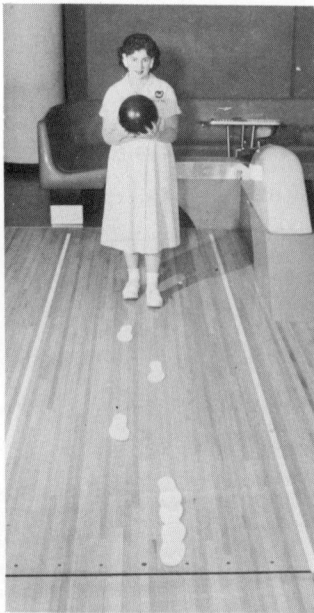

Foot patterns of the four-step approach.

A side view of my favored four-step delivery. Note the smooth action, full pushaway, and proper shoulder-level height of the backwing.

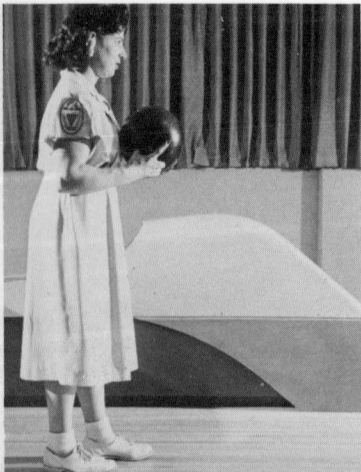

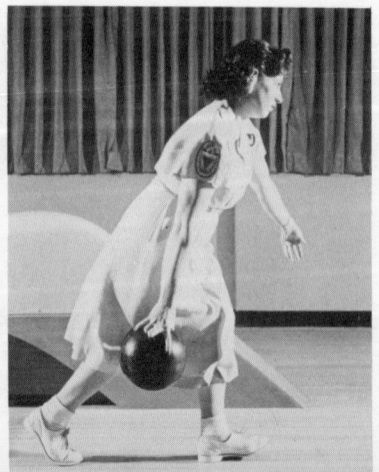

The less hurried motion, as compared with the three-step delivery, now becomes high-lighted. By the time the second step is taken with the left foot the ball is only starting down into the backswing. As I take my third step, my arm has reached the top of the backswing and is preparing for the sweeping delivery swing.

Now I am in position for a smooth, rhythmic delivery. My left foot takes its step and makes a full, deep slide toward the foul line, and the right foot maintains balance and acts as a brake. The slide will be anywhere from eight to sixteen inches, depending on your speed.

As I go into my slide, note that the ball is brought forward in a full pendulum swing. At this point the arm is kept close to the body and the wrist is straight and unbroken.

To improve your timing so that it becomes a rhythmic glide, try counting "one, two, three, slide," starting slowly and speeding up only slightly at the end.

A common fault among women is "breaking" the wrist as the ball is brought forward. The wrist should be in a straight-line position throughout the delivery for better action or "stuff" on the ball.

If you feel that your timing is off, following your pushaway, check the speed of the downswing. This is on the first step in the three-step delivery, the second step of the four-step delivery, or the third step of the five-step delivery. If your downswing is too fast and is throwing you off balance, cut down on your motion. This will not only help you to improve your timing but also will tend to keep the hand in the straight-line position.

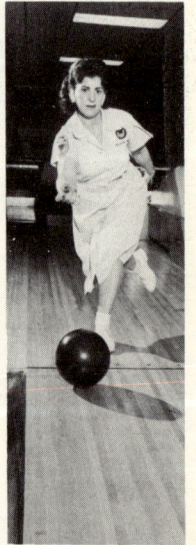

Front view of the four-step approach.

Front view of the five-step approach.

THE FIVE-STEP APPROACH   If you are an exceptionally tall woman, the shorter-stepped five-step delivery may be more suitable for you.

If you will look at the sequence photographs of the five-step delivery you will note that there is very little arm action on the short first step. This step simply gets the body into motion while maintaining balance. You have a choice of holding the ball still through that first step or else using a slightly downward or into the body motion.

Now as I go into the second step on the right foot the arm begins the pushaway. On the third step with the left foot, the ball follows the

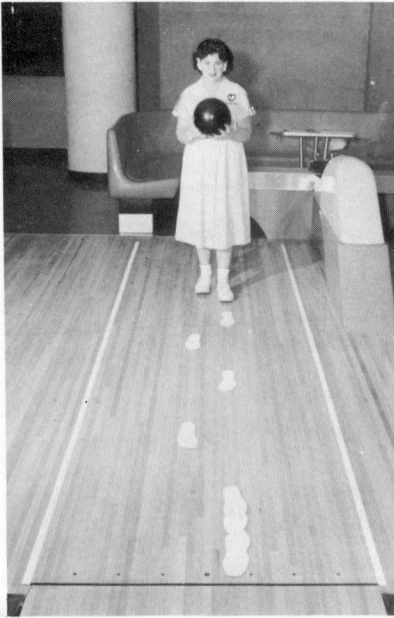

The five-step delivery foot pattern.

Here in the five-step delivery you will see that my first step is used merely to get the body in motion, the pushaway actually being delayed until the second step.

right leg into the downswing and on the fourth step on the right foot the ball continues to its maximum height of backswing and it only begins to come forward on the fifth step. The ball is delivered as I make the fifth step and slide on my left foot.

A study of the photos will demonstrate clearly how deliberate the whole action is in the five-step delivery.

There is one key danger if you decide to use the five-step delivery. You will find that you have an inclination to rush your first two steps. Remember, when using the five-step delivery, that you must keep it slow, smooth, and evenly paced to maintain your balance and rhythm.

FOLLOW-THROUGH Everything you have done properly will be ruined without a complete follow-through of the right arm as and after the ball is released.

Make sure that you bring the arm on through its delivery arc in a full, sweeping salute.

This keeps your ball on the line at which you are aiming. It also allows your ball to spin, and a spinning ball won't deflect as it contacts the pins the way a "dead" ball will.

To sum up my advice on delivery, I would suggest that you use the four-step approach and learn it from the outset. Use an easy pushaway and keep your steps measured and rhythmic. It is a time-honored axiom in bowling that a good bowler keeps her shoulders squared to the pins and the arm in close to the side. Make a deep slide on the left leg and follow through as the ball is delivered with a full, eye-level salute.

7 *Watch your backswing*

I PURPOSELY REFRAINED FROM MENTIONING THE HEIGHT TO WHICH THE backswing should be carried, while describing the approach, because I didn't want the delivery to seem too complicated.

The delivery is a simple process if you do it with easy rhythm, and that phase should be mastered before worrying about such refinements as the height of your backswing and proper release of the ball.

However, the secret of releasing the ball properly at the foul line is to bring the ball up just to the level of your shoulders on the backswing.

Many women do not get enough speed on their ball. The reason should be obvious. They simply haven't taken enough of a backswing. As I pointed out before, the backswing can be lengthened merely by giving the ball a stronger pushaway. Or you can add to your backswing simply by holding the ball a bit higher as you take your starting stance and letting the weight of the ball carry the arm into the backswing naturally. Of course, the maximum height of the backswing is shoulder level. However, it is not necessary for a woman to reach this particular height.

Either method will increase your swing and permit you to carry the ball higher on your backswing.

Conversely, if you are getting too much backswing, the ball can be held lower in the stance or you can use a smaller pushaway.

But the maximum height of the backswing is at shoulder level.

It is a good idea to have someone check the height of your backswing on frequent occasions to see that you are carrying the ball back neither too high nor too low.

A backswing that is too high means that you are trying to overpower the pins and, in the process, are ruining your timing and accuracy.

This is the optimum height for your backswing, but it is absolutely maximum.

If you drop the ball at your side like this, you aren't getting enough of a backswing. Use more pushaway.

A close-up of how the full, deep slide pays off

A backswing that is too low means that you aren't getting enough power into your ball and, in all probability, are dropping it at your side instead of laying it out over the foul line.

RELEASING THE BALL   This is the critical point of your delivery, with the ball coming forward as you start on your slide and being rolled well out over the foul line just as the slide is being completed in one sweeping, rhythmic movement.

The deep bend of the left knee pays off at this point. For only by sliding on a well-bent leg can you reach all the way out in front of you and roll the ball off your hand onto the alley bed. Remember that the ball is not "lofted" or thrown. The ball simply rolls off the fingers.

In recapping this phase of your game, bear in mind that the maximum backswing should be at shoulder level and you can regulate it up or down by holding the ball higher or lower or by varying the length of your pushaway.

Release the ball out over the foul line from a full, deep slide in which the shoulders are kept square to the pins. If you are "lofting" the ball too far out, your backswing is too high. If you are dropping the ball beside you, check your delivery. If you're not getting enough speed, your backswing probably isn't high enough.

as I roll the ball well out over the foul line.

A full-figure view of how far out on the lane the ball lands
even though I have finished up well behind the foul line.

8 *How I roll my professional hook-type ball*

In baseball there are any number of "pitches." In bowling there are only four. With a bit of practice you can roll any one of them, but I would suggest that you develop and stick to the hook ball which I and most of the other professionals use.

The three other types of ball are the straight ball, the curve ball, and the backup ball.

Of the four, the hook is the best for all general purposes even though the straight ball is easier to roll and, if you don't have time for practice, will give you better control in shooting for spares.

The pay-off ball, however, is the hook, and with a minimum of practice it will return great dividends. This type of ball, used by practically all the high-average stars, creates a wider storm center because of a twisting action which flips the pins into one another and thereby gives you greater strike action than you would get from a straight ball.

The curve ball, because of its great circle action, also will "mix" the pins greatly but it is much more difficult to steer and therefore I would not recommend it.

There is a great deal of disdain among high-average bowlers for the backup ball. This is due to the fact that the backup ball, because of its clockwise spin, will leave you with a greater percentage of splits.

Yet I have noticed that a great number of women roll the backup ball naturally and do fairly well with it. So, if you are a casual bowler with no time for practice, I would say you can enjoy yourself and do fairly well with the backup ball which comes naturally.

This is not to say that I am endorsing the backup ball. I have to hold, because of its greater pin-toppling percentage, that the explosive hook ball is the best. And I am quite certain that with the proper amount of practice you can develop a hook ball that will work consistently and pay off with much higher scores.

THE HOOK BALL   Actually the hook ball is not difficult to roll. As you will notice in the posed sequence pictures showing how I roll the hook, you merely "shake hands" with the ball. In other words, the "V" formed by thumb and forefinger comes out straight toward the target. Observe in particular that the forearm, wrist, and back of the hand all are kept in a straight line while I am making the delivery. This position is held throughout the follow-through for a full shake-hand salute.

This diagram illustrates how you play the hook ball to score a 1-3 pocket strike.

The hook-ball hand action, taken without the ball to demonstrate fully the "shake-hands" method of rolling what I consider the most effective type of ball.

One of the most difficult things you will have to learn is to deliver your ball at the same speed all the time. This is to ensure that your ball "breaks" in a reliable manner at the same time and the same distance. If I should deliver the ball at a faster speed than usual, the spin will not take as quickly and the "break" will be delayed. If I should roll the ball more slowly than usual, the spin will take more quickly and I will get a greater hook than usual. Only by rolling the ball at the same speed all the time will I get a hook on which I can depend to break exactly the same at all times.

The hook ball spinning in for a strike.

The ball hooks as it nears the pins for a very simple reason. Because you have brought the handshake straight through and up, your thumb leaves the ball first and, a fraction of a second later, your fingers automatically and without any effort on your part impart a counter-clockwise spin as they leave the ball. This is what produces your hook, the spin "taking hold" as the ball nears the pins.

Naturally, if you roll the ball at varied speeds, the spin will "take" sooner or later, depending on the speed, and your hook will react differently all the time. But if delivered at a constant speed with the thumb to the side, your hook will break in a dependable manner. The position of the thumb to the side also determines the amount of the hook. Aimed at the 3 pin, or at the 6 pin if you are getting a bigger hook, it breaks right into the 1-3 pocket.

THE STRAIGHT BALL   There are those who contend that, because the straight ball is the easiest to roll, the beginner should use this type of ball. This probably is sensible if you are only going to bowl once in a while because, as I have said previously, it will make your spare shooting a bit easier.

In the accompanying sequence photos you will see clearly how I deliver this ball. Throughout this delivery, you will observe, the palm is kept underneath the ball. As in all the deliveries, the arm is brought through in a full, pendulum sweep and the ball merely rolls off the upturned palm.

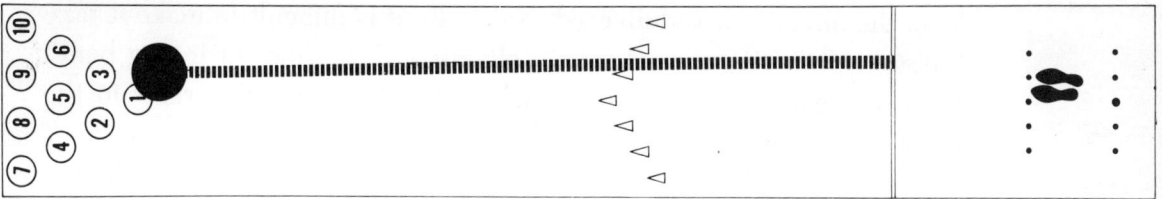

Diagram showing how the straight ball travels in scoring a strike.

In delivering the straight ball, the hand comes through with the palm up as the ball rolls off the fingers.

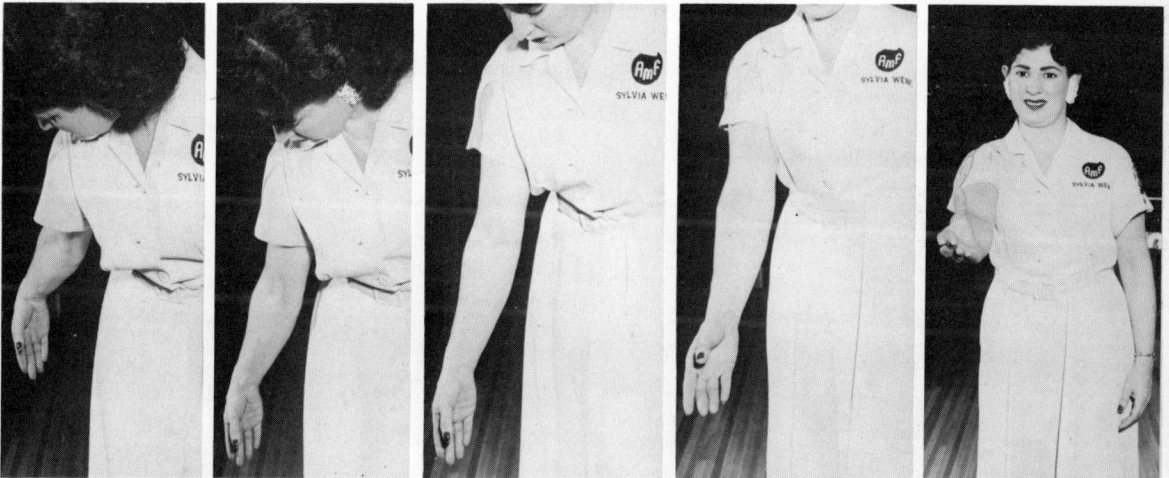

The straight ball driving into the 1-3 pocket for a clean strike.

You must be absolutely certain, as the ball is released, that you do not twist the wrist to one side or the other. A twist to the right will give the ball backup action, and a twist to the left will impart curving action.

When shooting for a strike with the straight ball, it is played from the right side of the alley. The ball is aimed at the 1-3 pocket and, because the straight ball deflects rather easily owing to its lack of driving spin, the hit should be "high" on the head pin.

THE CURVE BALL   Whereas the hook ball travels in a straight path before the hook spin "grabs" and makes the ball cut in sharply, the curve ball is simply what its name implies. It travels in a long, curving arc from the moment it is delivered. Naturally it is difficult to make it take the same sweeping arc on every delivery and, because of its big bend, it has a greater "pick" factor which makes it particularly risky in the shooting of spares.

The curve ball is the direct result of an exceptionally slow delivery.

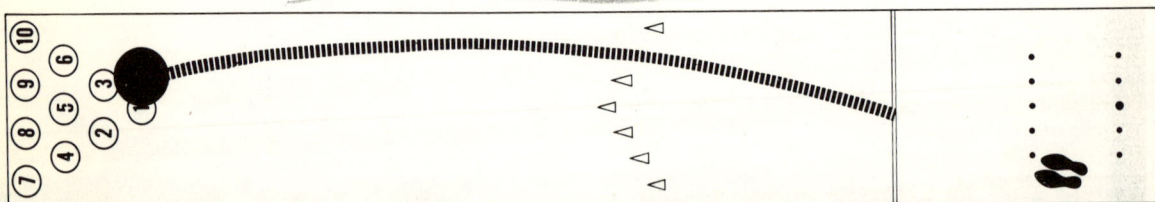

Diagram illustrating how the sweeping curve ball must be played to finish up in the 1-3 pocket.

Here we have the counter-clockwise turning of the hand in delivering the curve ball. Note the difference between this finish and the finish of the hook ball.

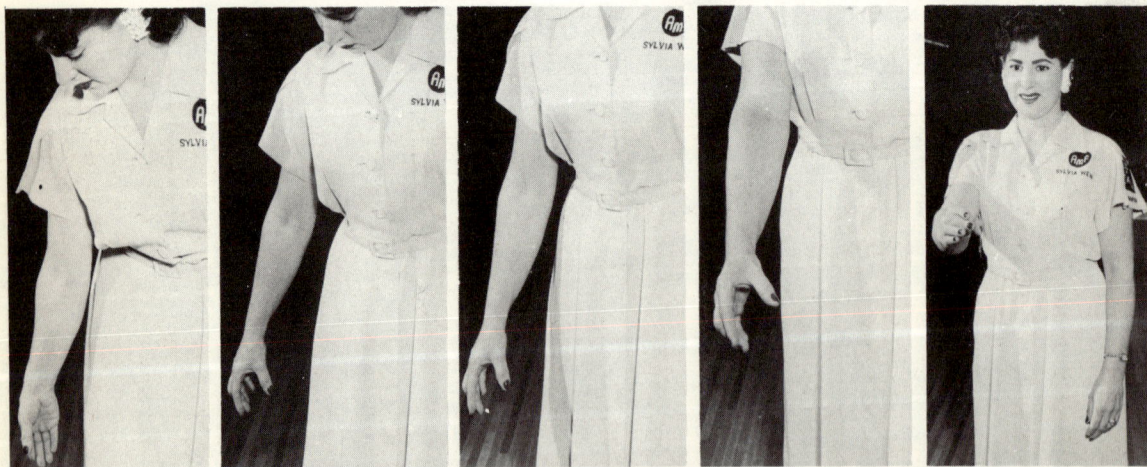

How the curve ball, while difficult to control, whirls the pins off the lane in a strike hit.

Because the ball is laid down slowly, the spin takes effect at once and the result is a slow, long, lazy curve.

In the accompanying photos, you will note that the curve ball is delivered with a decided wrist break. Also, as I release the ball, you will observe that I give the wrist a flip-over "lift" to increase the normal spin which the fingers would naturally give it.

If you deliver a curve ball, and like its spectacular action, remember that it is delivered from the center of the lane and out toward the right-hand gutter. About halfway down the lane it will roundhouse inward and on into the 1-3 pocket. But, as I said, it calls for great geometrical precision without paying any great dividends.

THE BACKUP BALL If you are delivering a backup—and can't understand why—a close look at the sequence pictures will tell you what you are doing. As you will see, you are simply flipping your hand and wrist over in a clockwise manner as you release the ball.

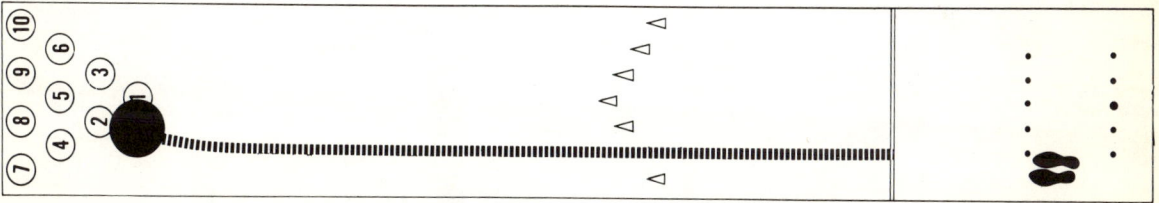

This diagram shows the path of the backup ball in scoring a strike in the 1-2 pocket.

What you are doing if you roll the backup ball. It's the straight-ball start but you are giving your hand a clockwise flip as you release the ball.

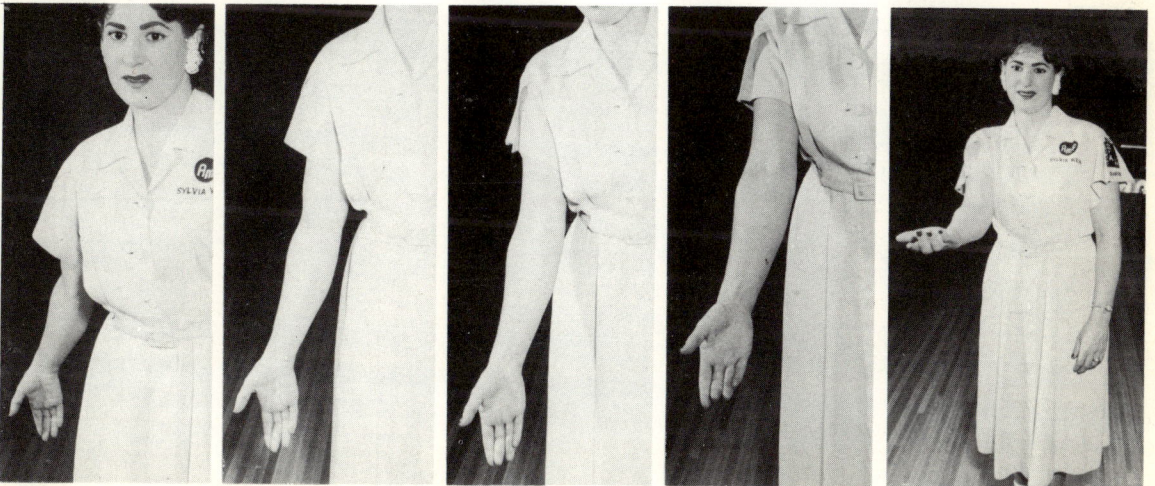

The backup is a ball which, because of its clockwise spin, hooks from left to right. Therefore it must be played into the 1-2 pocket for best results. But you will discover that almost any kind of full hit, meaning one which is too close to the head pin, will leave a great percentage of distressing splits.

It is a temptation, when you ordinarily use a sharp-breaking hook ball, to try the backup ball when faced with the tough 10-pin spare. Don't do it. Concentrate on perfecting your regular ball and you will find that, when you have developed consistency, it will make any spare setup you face.

Take a tip from me and develop a hook ball which you roll with the same speed at all times whether you are shooting a strike or a spare. This will give you a constant "break" on which you can depend. And in the long run it will pay off with appreciably higher scores.

The action of the backup ball as it scores a strike in the 1-2 pocket.

My secrets for shooting spares **9**

STRIKES ARE THE BIG THRILL OF BOWLING. BUT GETTING YOUR SPARES consistently is what will pay off with a higher average.

I have two big secrets for shooting spares:

1. I concentrate even more, if such a thing is possible, when shooting a spare than I do in going for a strike.

2. I use a cross-alley system generally to make certain that the pins are "covered" better.

It should be obvious why you must concentrate even more on your spare shot than when you are faced with the full set of pins. On a strike ball, if you hit anywhere near the head pin, you will get the majority of the pins. Then, if you had what appeared to be a good hit and left one or more pins standing, you are apt to feel let down. So you must re-gear yourself mentally to go after that spare with everything you have.

Now you are faced with a demanding shot with which you must hit a certain spot exactly. You'll be surprised, when you concentrate, how you will cut down on your misses.

Then there is the added factor of giving yourself the best of the percentages by rolling your spares from an angle that will reduce your chances of "picking" one pin.

My system, and the one used by most high-average bowlers, is the cross-alley technique. This simply means shooting left-side spares, say the 7 pin, from the right side of the approach. Conversely, you shoot right-side spares, such as the 10 pin, from the left side of the approach —angling your ball across the lane.

Right here I'd like to caution you against moving out of your own lane. I have seen bowlers who, when shooting the 10 pin for example, will move clear over onto the next approach to their left.

You should never move off of your own approach. To emphasize this point, in the accompanying photos you will see that I have run masking tape from the edge of the gutters clear back to the end of the approach. In one you will note my regular strike position. Then you will see the extreme position to which I move to the left in shooting spares on the right side and the extreme position to which I move to the right in

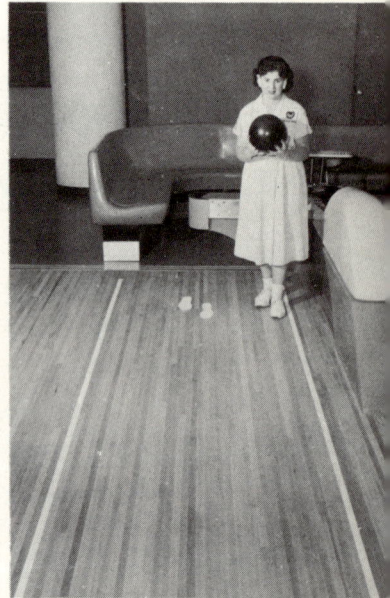

Left. My normal position in shooting for a strike. *Center.* I move to the right side of the approach to shoot a left-side spare such as the 7 pin. The cutouts show my normal strike position. *Right.* Here I have moved to the left side of the approach to shoot a right-side spare such as the 10 pin.

shooting spares on the left side. Observe that in no case do I move outside the width of my own approach.

In this connection, you don't even have to leave your own lane to check your spare setup. How many times have you seen someone walk over onto an adjoining lane, craning her neck to see whether there is a "sleeper" pin, such as when the 1-5 or 3-9 setups are left? If you get in the habit of using the Pindicator, located just above the pit, it will show you just which pins are there, as Carol Christensen is pointing out in the accompanying photo.

Carol Christensen shows how the Pindicator, over the pits, tells you just what pins are left in your spare setup.

SPARES ON THE LEFT SIDE   The best way to shoot your spares is illustrated graphically in this chapter with a chart of the various setups you will face and an accompanying photo showing just how the ball should make contact to avoid costly "picks,"—shots that pick off one or more pins but leave one or more still standing.

When your ball isn't working in properly to the head pin you will see a lot of the 1-2-4 and 1-2-4-7 setups. The 1-2-4 can be made from the 1-3 pocket but I prefer to make this one, and the 1-2-4-7, by crossing over the head pin for a Brooklyn or Jersey hit which will sweep all the pins and leave less chance for a "pick."

Remembering that these are shot from the right-hand side of the approach, let's look at the 1-2-4-10. This is another cross-over shot because the head pin must be knocked over to take out the 10 pin.

You will face such setups as the 2-4-5 and the 2-4-5-8 after a light pocket hit. You can't miss the 2-4-5 if you hit the 2 pin fairly full on either side. But if you are throwing a hook ball, on the 2-4-5-8 you must come into the 2-5 pocket so that your ball will carry through and take the 8 pin.

You can make the 2-4-7 and 4-7 leaves from the right side of the 2 pin but here again, as shown in the accompanying graphs and illustrations, you cover the setup best by crossing over to make sure you don't hit the 2 pin too "thin" and thus get a "pick." If you cross over and get a "thin" hit on the left side of the 2 pin it won't make any difference, so you can see that the percentages are with you if you cross over on both setups.

When you are faced with the 2-7 "baby" split, you play exactly the same type of cross-over shot as you would for the 2-4-7 setup. Crossing over the 2 pin will deflect your ball on over to the 7 pin. Play this shot with the same confidence as if the 4 pin were there, and you'll be surprised at your percentage of conversions.

Three other splits which you play from the right side of the approach are the 4-5, the 4-9, and the 5-10. Naturally they call for pin-point control and here, again, confidence is as important as anything else. In shooting the 4-5 you have to fit your ball in between them. But on the 4-9 and 5-10 you once again cross over the front pin.

Making the 1-2-4.

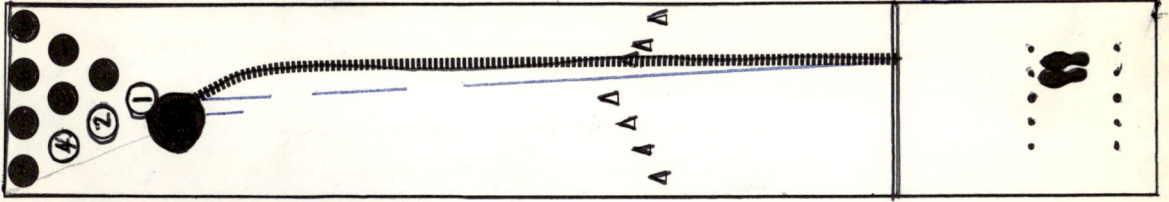

Crossing the head pin on the 1-2-4-7.

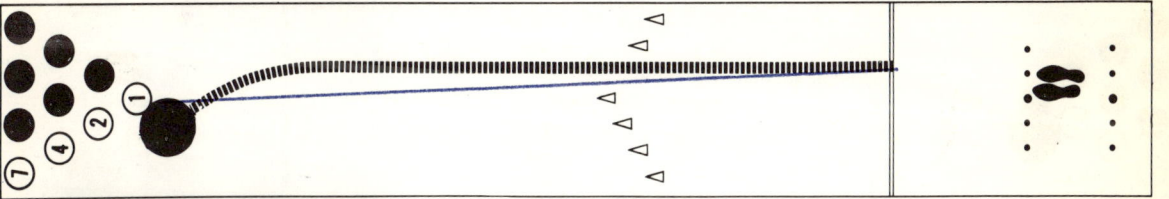

The cross-over gives the head pin a chance at the 10.

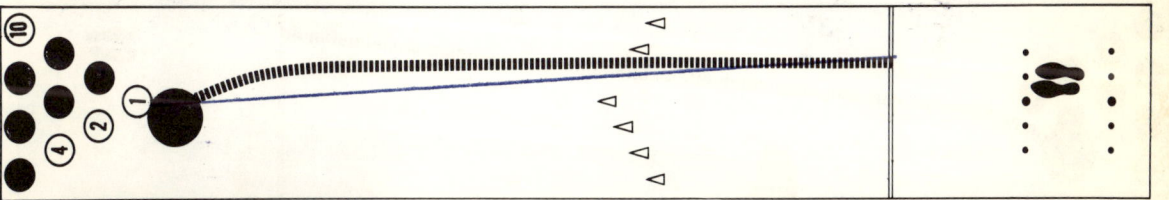

The 2-5 pocket is your best bet here.

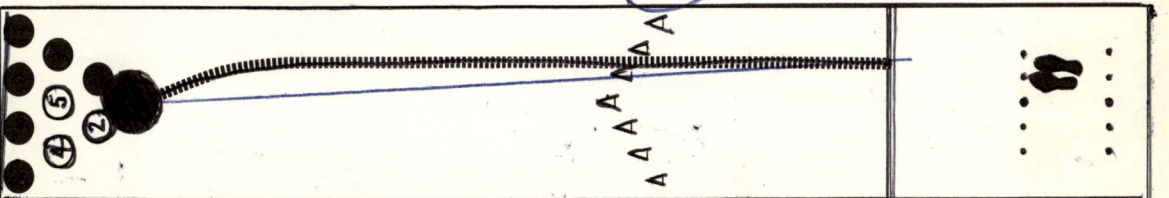

Don't hit the 2 pin too light or you'll get a "pick."

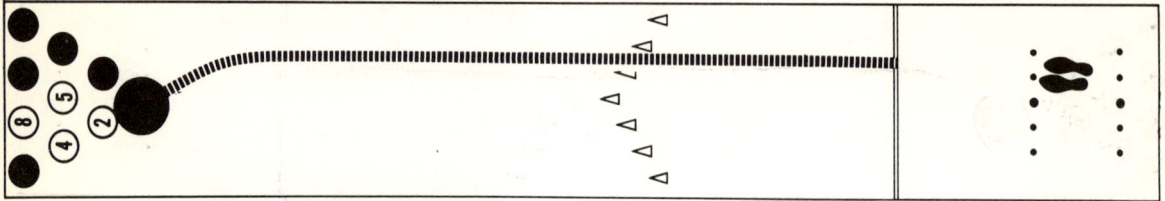

The thin hit in this picture threatens a "pick."

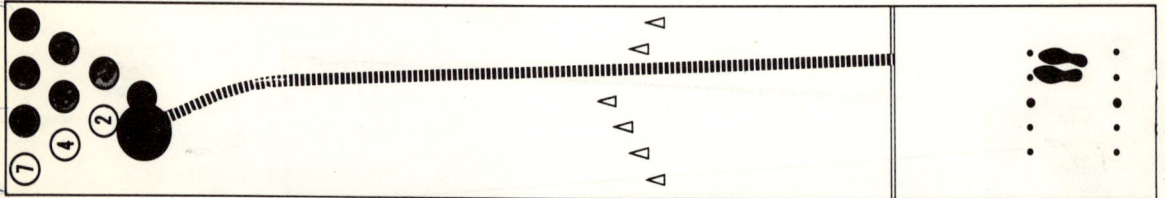

This is the safe side for the 4-7 shot.

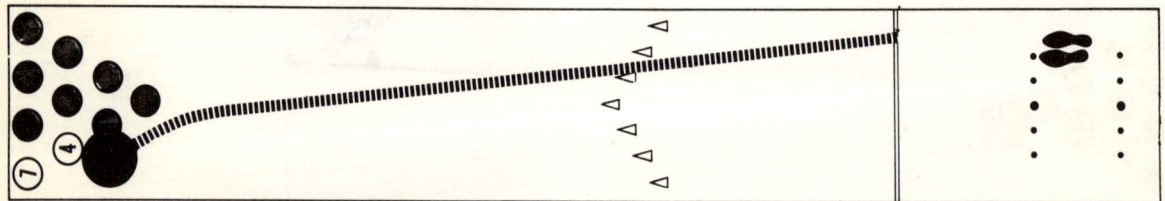

This hook ball makes the 2-7 "baby" split look easy.

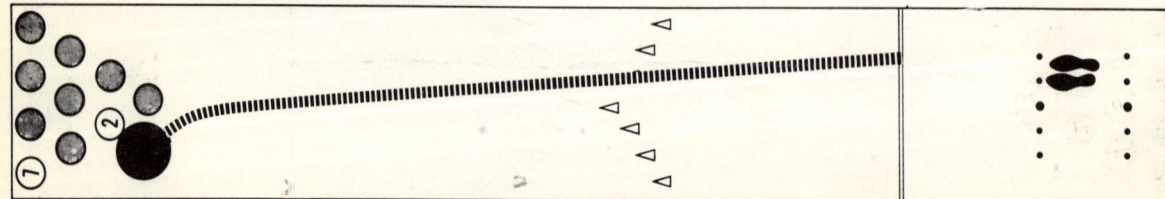

Hooking in from the right side to convert the 4-5 split.

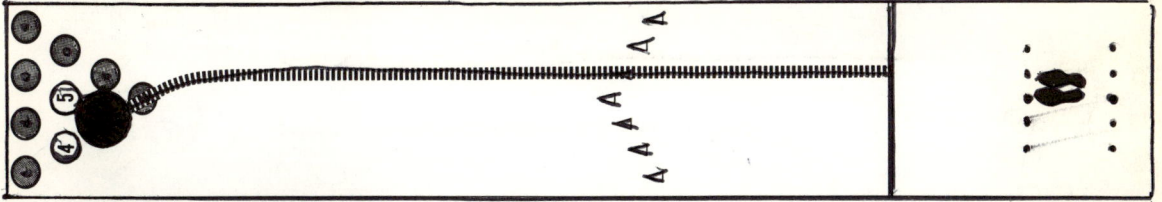

The 4-9 is made from the right side of the approach.

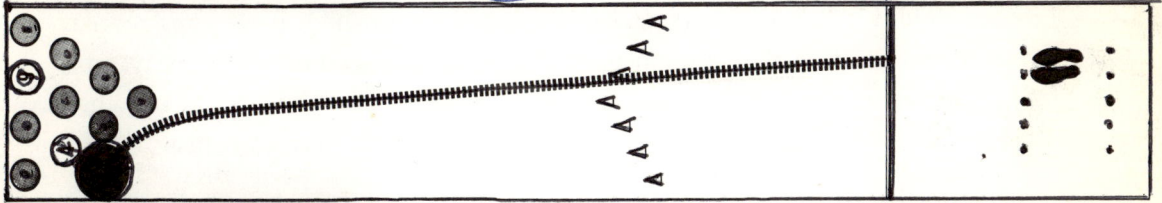

Sliding the 5 pin over to get the 10.

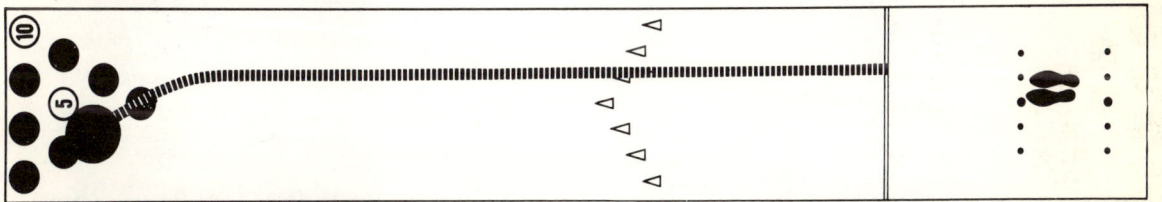

You can shoot this tough one from your regular strike position.

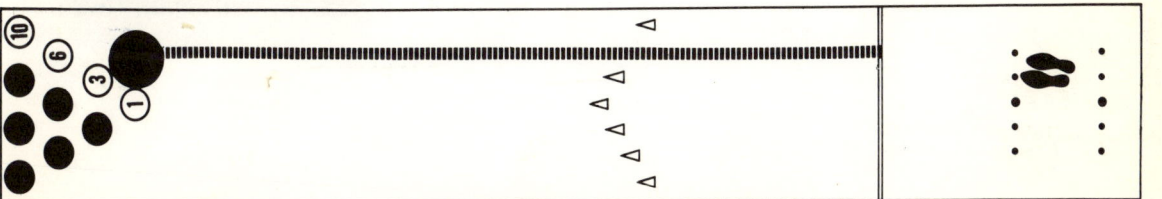

Here again you can use your regular strike spot but you have a better percentage from the left-hand side of the approach.

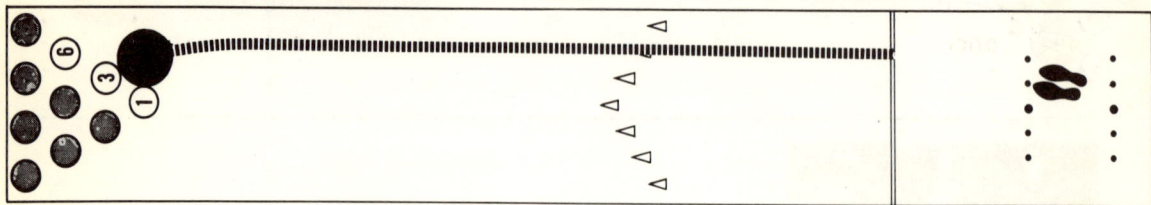

SPARES ON THE RIGHT SIDE Now we move to the left side of the approach as we take our stance.

There are two right-side leaves that you can shoot from your regular strike position if you choose, as shown in the accompanying diagrams. These are the 1-3-6-10 and the 1-3-6 spare shots which are set up when your strike ball crosses the head pin too much and you miss it completely.

There are some who believe it is better to shoot either of these setups from the left side of the approach. Aim at the 1-3 pocket and, even if your ball goes straight through, the 3 pin will take out the 6 and 10 pins. Shooting the 1-3-6 cross-alley also cuts down your margin for error and eliminates a certain "pick" hazard if you should hit the head pin too full.

The same cross-alley angle is used for the 3-6-10 and the 6-10 spares. If you shoot it down the right-hand side of the lane your chances of a "pick" are increased. But if you cross the front pin from the left-hand side as shown in the diagrams you can't miss.

You shoot the 3-10 "baby" split in the same way that you would the 3-6-10, trying to forget that the 6 pin is missing. Merely shoot from the left side of the approach as if hitting into the 3-6 pocket and the ball will deflect off into the 10 pin. You also can make it if you hit the 3 pin on the left side, but this is increasing your chances of a "pick."

I also shoot the 3-5-6-9 and the 5-9 spares from the left side of the approach. Here I try for a full hit in the 3-6 pocket so that again there will be less chance of a "pick."

Splits which I shoot from the left side of the approach include the 5-7, the 6-7, and the 6-7-10. Prospects for sliding that 5 pin over, in the 5-7 setup, are better if you hook your ball in from the left side of the approach.

These are the most difficult shots you will face and, when shooting the 6-7 and 6-7-10, you should make certain to get the 6 pin or the 6-10 rather than chance missing them all in a vain try to convert the split. You will get the 6-10 setup best from the left-hand side of the approach and, with a lot of luck, you may pull off the carom shot which picks up the 7 pin for a spare.

You'll need another precision shot from the left-hand side of the approach to make the 5-6 "fit-in" split, a shot in which you hook in off the 6 pin.

Give the charts a bit of study and you'll soon discover that the high-average bowler is playing the law of averages by angling for his spares. Just shoot them cross-alley, the right-hand spares from the left side of the approach and the left-hand spares from the right side of the approach, and at least you'll be giving yourself the best of it and avoiding a lot of costly "picks."

Shoot cross-alley from the left-hand side of the approach to really cover the 3-6-10.

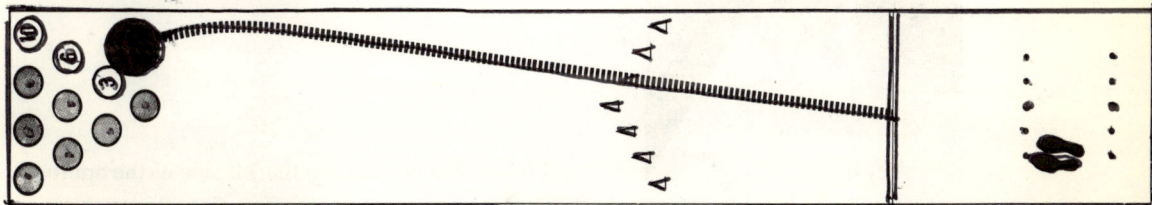

You can "pick" this from the right side, so cover it better from the left side of the approach.

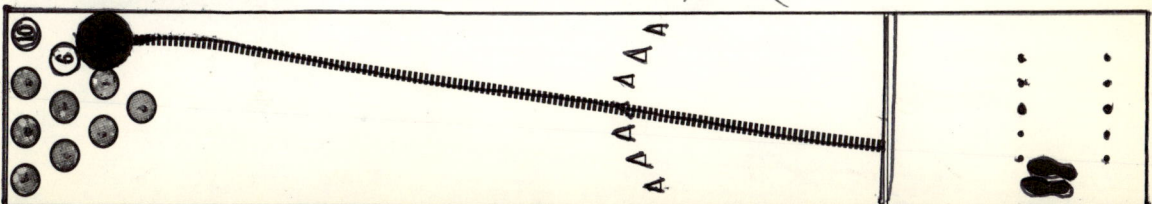

Forget that the 6 pin is missing and, bowling from the left side, hit the 3 pin thin.

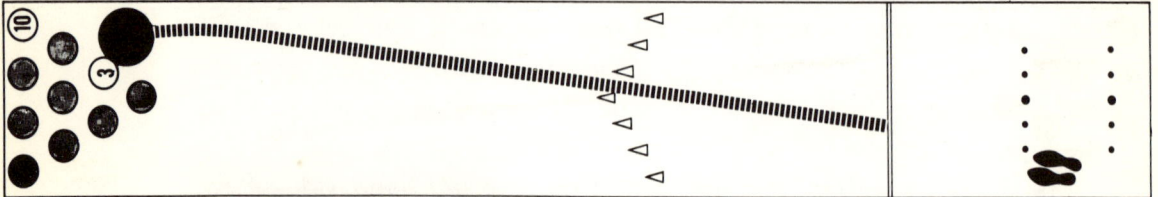

Let your hook come in for a full 3-6 pocket hit to get the 9 pin.

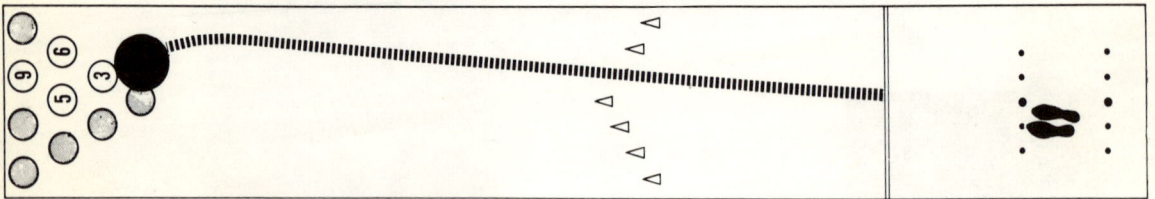

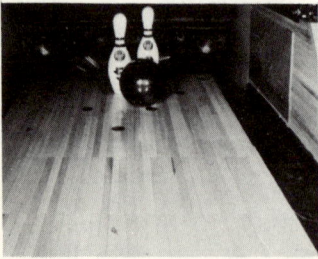

Hook this one in from the left side of the approach.

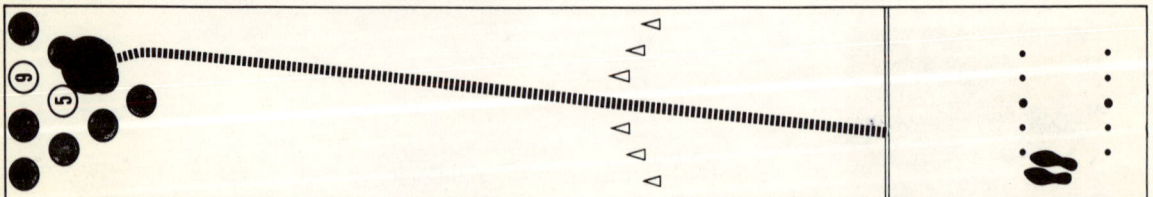

Your chances of making the tough 5-7 split are better from the left side of the approach.

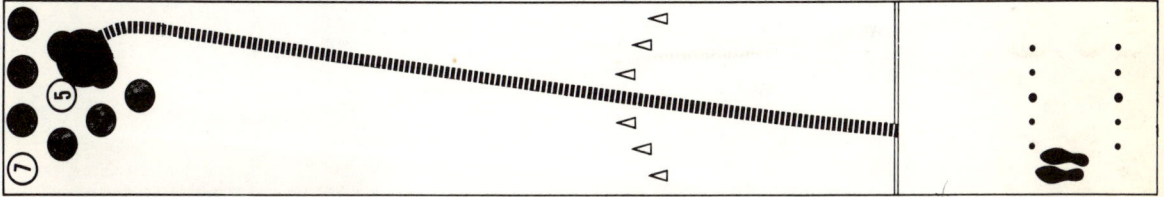

Shooting cross-alley is your best hope here.

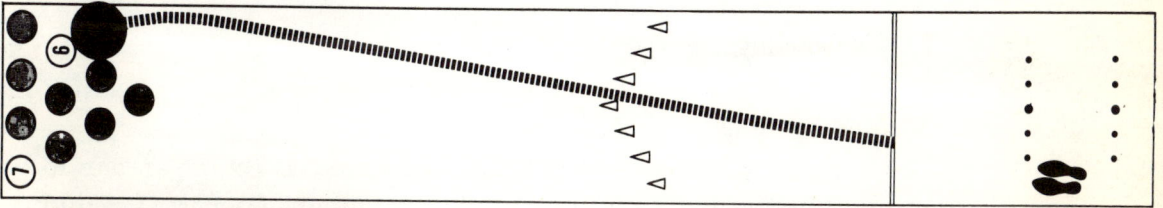

This calls for a perfect "fit-in" shot from the left side of the approach.

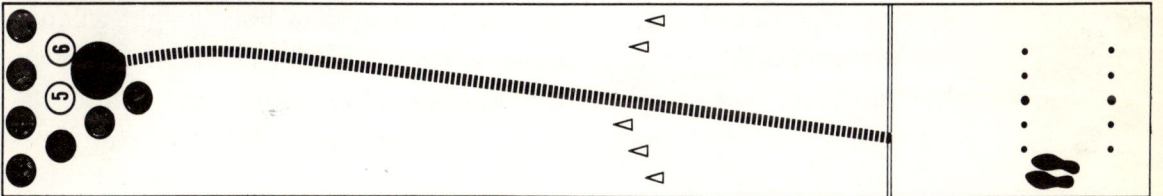

10 *A guide to perfect aiming*

IT STANDS TO REASON THAT, ONCE YOU HAVE MASTERED YOUR DELIVERY, you still won't get any consistent results by merely firing away blindly. If you are firing a gun, you must use the gun sights to hit your target. In other words, you must take aim.

This holds in bowling, too, only here we have three different ways in which to zero in on your target. These are:

1. Pin bowling.
2. Spot bowling.
3. Line bowling.

You will find vehement exponents of each method. Yet the answer to their effectiveness is that each is used by top-flight bowlers. I would suggest that you try them all and find out by trial and error which suits you individually. Once you have decided, however, stick to that one method of aiming.

PIN BOWLING   Users of this system simply keep their eyes on the pins when delivering the ball.

To use this system, you look straight at the 1-3 pocket from your starting stance and imagine a line drawn along your line of sight when bowling for a strike. Then, with your eyes on the 1-3 pocket, you follow that imaginary line straight to the foul line in delivering your ball.

This is a delivery I would suggest only for those who roll a straight ball.

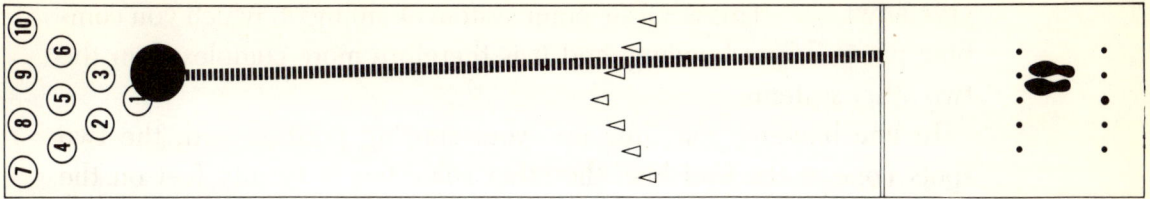

In pin bowling, you keep your eyes on your target throughout your delivery.

SPOT BOWLING This is the system which I use and which is used most generally by high-average bowlers.

You will notice that the alley bed out beyond the foul line is constructed of thin boards which run lengthwise down the lane. In their finishing and polishing these boards most often are of different colors. This makes it easy to select one of these boards and then to concentrate on rolling your ball over it.

If your ball breaks in too much to the head pin, you simply try one or more boards to your right. If your ball isn't getting "up" to the head pin, merely take another board more to the left.

Another phase of spot bowling is to line up your starting position with some spot out on the lane. Your ball then is rolled out over that spot. The danger of the one-spot system is that even the slightest change in your starting position will change the angle at which you roll your ball over the one spot.

I would suggest, therefore, that you select one spot at the foul line and another some ten to twenty feet out on the lane. But of course you look at the one spot ten to twenty feet out on the lane throughout the entire delivery and until after the ball rolls over it. Concentrate on rolling your ball over those two spots. Adjustments can be made as necessary, to the right or left of the more distant spot, to take your ball into the pocket.

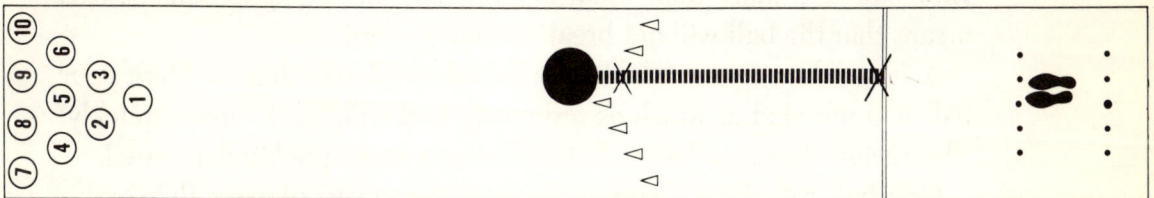

In spot bowling, pick out a spot at the foul line and one fifteen feet out on the lane and roll the ball over both spots.

LINE BOWLING   This is a four-point system of aiming in which you combine pin and spot bowling, and it is therefore more complex than the two other systems.

In line bowling you "line up" your starting position with the two spots (one at the foul line, the other some ten to twenty feet on the lane) and the 1-3 pocket. Gauge an imaginary line between these three spots with full concentration on the spot ten to twenty feet out on the lane, and follow this imaginary line throughout your delivery.

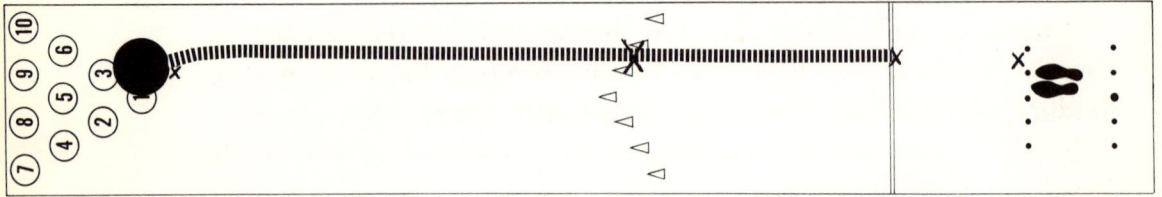

There are four check points in line bowling: the starting position, spots at the foul line and fifteen feet out, and finally the pocket.

Personally, I would recommend the two-spot system as being the least complicated and most effective. If your spot at the foul line and the one ten to twenty feet out on the lane are aligned properly it stands to reason that concentrating on rolling over those two points will put you in the proper starting position and make your ball wind up on target.

ADJUSTING TO THE LANE   You will learn with increasing annoyance that all lanes are different.

Some are "fast" and others are "slow," which means that your ball will react differently.

A "fast" lane is one which, because it is highly polished, will make your ball skid more than usual before the spin begins to "take." This means that the ball will not break as much as ordinarily.

A "slow" lane is one which is polished to a lesser degree. Here your ball will not skid as much as ordinarily and will "grab" more quickly. This means that your ball will start hooking more quickly than usual.

One ball rolled on a strange lane, if the speed of your delivery is constant, will tell you whether the lane is normal, "fast," or "slow."

Should your ball work as it normally does, no adjustments of any great consequence will be necessary.

However, if your ball is not getting "up" to the head pin on the first few rolls but instead is hitting too full on the 3 pin, you know that the lane is "fast" and so polished that your spin isn't taking as quickly as it normally does.

The answer is that you must move your starting position to the right. You also must move your starting spot at the foul line fractionally to the right so that your angle now will be more toward the head pin. Still using the same spot out on the lane, you now will find your ball getting "up" to the head pin even though your spin is taking longer to "grab" and the ball isn't breaking as much as it usually does.

Similarly, your first ball, if delivered at your normal speed, will tell you that you are on a "slow" lane if the ball dives over and across the head pin. A bigger hook than you normally get tells you that the spin is taking effect sooner than ordinarily.

In this case you must adjust your starting position by moving more toward the left or the center of the lane, although it is important to bear in mind that you should never deliver your strike ball from the left of the lane center. On a "slow" lane simply move your foul-line spot fractionally to the left, and this new angle on your second sighting spot out on the lane will provide more room for your ball to hook.

In some cases the lane will be so "fast" that you still won't be getting enough hook. In this case simply give a slower delivery, which can be effected by using less pushaway. And, if you still are getting too much hook, you can obtain the faster delivery necessary by employing a fuller pushaway.

Another important factor when rolling on "fast" or "slow" lanes is to keep in mind their peculiarities when shooting spares. Allow more room for your ball to "break" on a "slow" lane, and play your shots finer on a "fast" lane where your ball will not break as much as usual.

11 *The way you keep score*

A FEW BASIC SYMBOLS DENOTE THE VARIOUS PIN SETUPS, AND ONCE YOU have learned these, scoring becomes quite easy.

The game is divided into ten boxes or "frames." Each frame represents one turn for the bowler.

In each frame you are given two shots to get all the pins. However, only one ball is needed if you roll a "strike," the term used to indicate that you have knocked down all ten pins with your first ball. If you require two balls to get all ten pins, this means you have made a "spare."

In keeping score you use a set of established symbols, and once you have mastered them you will be able to go back over your game and reconstruct every shot you made.

The new score sheets have a large box for your total score in each frame plus two smaller boxes in the upper right-hand corner of each box to designate what happened on each of the two balls delivered in that frame. It is in these smaller boxes that the symbols are written to show how you arrived at your cumulative score marked in the larger box.

These different symbols are illustrated in the isolated frames. For example, in the frame marked "1," you have the symbol for a strike. This symbol, placed in the small upper left-hand box, is an "X."

In the isolated frame marked "2" you have the symbol for a spare, designating the fact that all the pins were knocked down with two balls. The first of the small boxes shows that you made nine pins on your first ball and the spare sign in the second small box designates that you made the spare by, in this case, getting the one remaining pin with your second ball.

The third isolated frame shows a converted split for a spare. Here you made eight pins on your first ball, as shown in the first small box, but left yourself a split. When a pin is down in the middle of a spare series, such as the 6 pin falling between the 3 and 10 pins, or when you have two pins left standing in the same row, such as the 4-5 or 5-6, you have what is called a "split." When you make a split it becomes a spare, designated in the third frame with a line through the zero denoting the split. The fourth frame merely shows a split which was not made, after getting seven pins on the first ball.

1	2	3	4	5	6
Strike symbol.	A spare.	Converted split.	Missed split.	A miss.	Foul on first ball.

1	2	3	4	5	6	7	8	9	10	TOTAL
8	28	45	52	72	90	107	114	143	163	163

A complete game. Scoring of this game, step by step, is described fully in this chapter.

In the fifth isolated frame you have the marking for a miss, after getting six pins on the first ball. Then, in the sixth isolated frame, you see the marking for a foul on the first ball. Note here that a spare was made on the second ball by knocking down all the pins. But the fact that all the pins were made on the one shot doesn't count as a strike because it was your second ball.

Now that you have learned the various symbols, look at the chart which shows you the scoring of a full game.

Let's run through it, frame by frame.

Frame 1: You knock down eight pins on your first ball, as shown in the first small box, and miss with your second ball. Therefore you have 8 in your first frame, which is written into the large box.

Frame 2: You have a strike with your first ball. So now let's consider the scoring on a strike and a spare. When you strike, you get the added total of 10 for that ball plus the total count on your next two balls. On a spare, you get the total of 10 for your spare plus the total pins on your next ball only. Thus, when you strike in the second frame, you don't add your score until you have rolled two more balls.

Frame 3: You knock down nine pins on your first ball—but still do not fill in the second frame total because your strike there gets the next TWO balls. So you bowl your second ball in the third frame and make your spare. Now you have had two balls to go with the strike in the second frame, and the strike and the two-ball spare add up to 20 pins. This is added to your first frame total of 8 and you have 28 in the second frame.

Frame 4: You knock down seven pins with your first ball, leaving a split. Going back to the still open third frame, where you had a spare, you add those 7 pins on your first ball to the 10 pins for your spare, a total of 17, which is added to 28 in your second frame, to give you 45 in the third frame. Now, on your second ball in the fourth frame, you miss all three pins in the split, so you have a total of 7 pins for the frame, which runs your total to 52.

Frame 5: You get a strike on your first ball. The big box is left open because now you are "working" on another bit of two-ball addition.

Frame 6: You get nine pins on your first ball but still don't tally up the fifth-frame score because you are "working" on a strike and get ten pins plus two balls. On your second ball you get the remaining pin for a spare. Now you add 20 points in the fifth big box, 10 for the strike and 10 for the spare, to run your fifth-frame total to 72.

Frame 7: You are "working" on a sixth-frame spare. So when you get eight on your first ball, you fill in the sixth-frame score of 10 for the spare and 8 for the first ball in the seventh frame, giving you 90 in the sixth. You have a split in the seventh, as noted in the second small box, and you make both pins for a spare.

Frame 8: You knock down seven pins with your first ball, as noted in the first small box. That lets you fill in the seventh frame, where your spare (10) plus 7 on your first ball gives you 17 to be added to 90 for a seventh-frame total of 107. Then, on your second ball, you miss the three pins. So you add the 7 for that frame, to give you 114 in the eighth frame.

Frame 9: You strike on your first ball and so have two more balls to add before filling in your score at that point.

Frame 10: You lead off with a strike. This gives you two more balls. You get nine pins with your second ball. Now you fill in the open ninth frame, 10 points for each of the two strikes plus 9 points, giving you 29 points and a ninth-frame total of 143.

Now, on the third ball of the last frame, and your last roll, you get the one remaining pin. This means you have added 20 points in the last frame, on a strike and a spare, giving you a grand total of 163.

All of this may appear somewhat confusing to begin with, but don't shy away from the scoring table. If you memorize the symbols and the general procedure, it will take only one or two actual games to give you complete mastery of score keeping.

12 *Mind your bowling manners*

BOWLING HAS COME A LONG WAY SINCE THE DAYS OF ITS ORIGIN AS A national sport. There was a time when it was held in low esteem, but now it is a sport for ladies and gentlemen. So remember that gracious behavior is as necessary on the bowling lanes as it is elsewhere.

The game has developed a definite code of good behavior. Observing this code of courtesy might, or might not, improve your bowling, but it certainly will make you much more popular.

The American Bowling Congress has drawn up a code of "do's" and "don'ts" which Carol Christensen and I illustrate in this chapter.

The A.B.C.'s list of "do's" include:

1. Do let the person on the right shoot first so that you won't disturb each other by racing to the foul line simultaneously.

2. Do be ready to bowl when it is your turn so that you won't unnecessarily delay the progress of the game.

3. Do eliminate such annoying and time-wasting motions as scraping of the feet, endless drying of the hands, and interminable posing when getting ready to make your shot.

4. Do restrain your "bench jockeying" when your opponent is preparing to shoot.

5. Do act graciously at all times, win or lose.

You can also see Carol and me acting out the "don'ts" in the accompanying photographs. These "don'ts" include:

1. Don't wear street shoes on the lanes. Skid marks left by rubber heels have caused more than one bowler to come to an abrupt halt while attempting to slide and suffer a painful fall.

2. After you have delivered your ball, don't linger at the foul line contemplating your setup because it is distracting to the person preparing to bowl on the adjacent lane.

3. Don't "body English" out of your own lane. You may collide with another bowler and somebody could be hurt by the ball she is delivering.

4. Don't wander heedlessly off your own approach when returning from the foul line. Again someone could be hurt.

5. Don't use another's ball. It is not only irritating to the owner but it slows down play. Even if the ball in question belongs to the house, the proper procedure is for the person who uses the ball first to continue using it just as if it belonged to her.

As the A.B.C. points out, all these rules are based on simple good manners. Obeying them will make bowling more fun for all concerned.

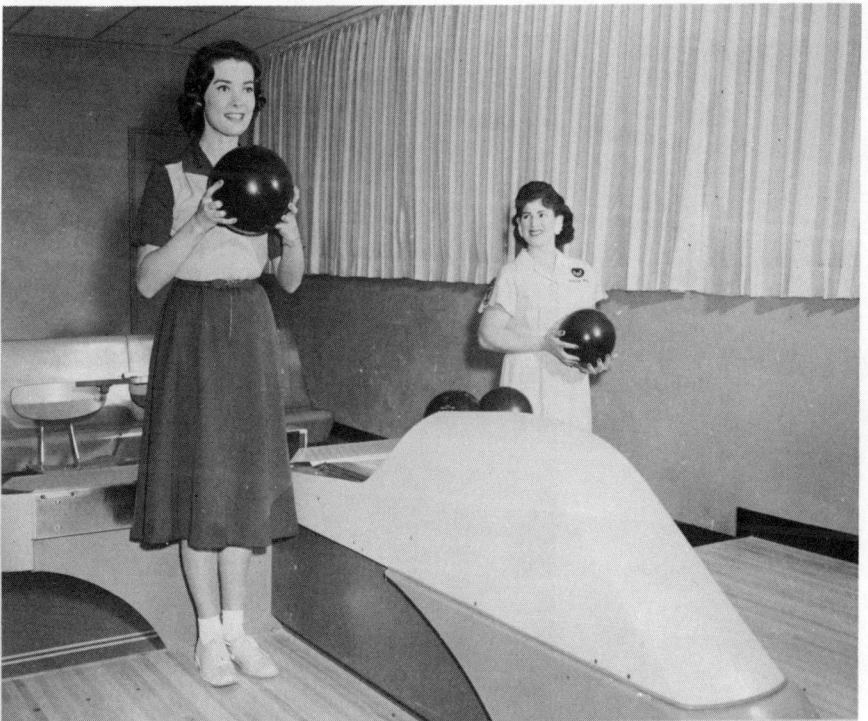

The bowler on the right rolls first. Courtesy demands that you wait out of her line of vision.

Don't linger needlessly contemplating your setup. You will be holding up play.

Don't "body English" into another lane. You could be injured.

Don't wander needlessly. It is dangerous as well as up-
setting to others.

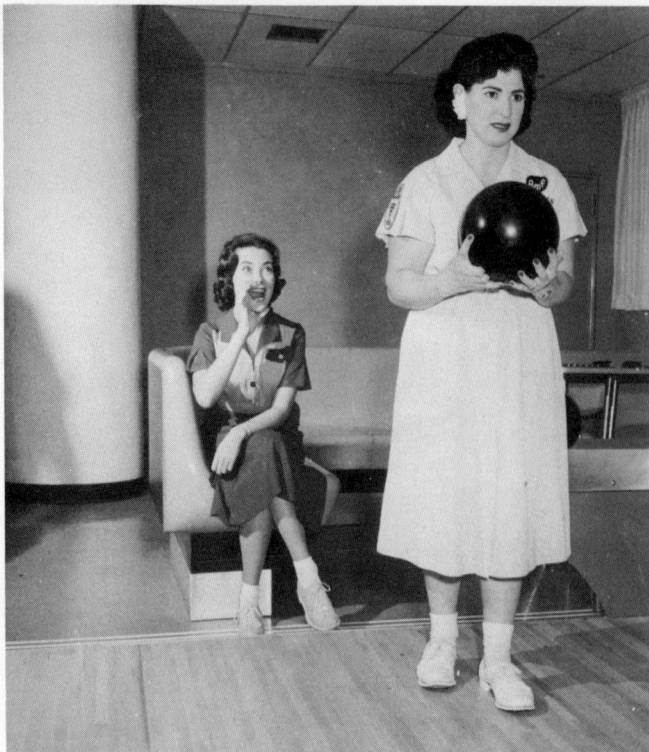

This kind of "bench talk" isn't sporting.

Keep your shoes clean and don't bowl with rubber heels. It marks the lane approaches like this and could cause a fall.

Bowling beauty tips **13**

A WOMAN IS KNOWN BY THE AURA OF FEMININITY THAT SURROUNDS HER. Her perfume, feminine daintiness, and make-up help to make her even more lovely.

Sometimes, in the rush of daily living, we forget some of the details we should remember. But an afternoon or evening of bowling should be something special. So take those few extra seconds to double check.

Wear a light, appealing fragrance, one that whispers and one definitely that doesn't shout. Work out a special make-up, one that is easy to apply, keeps you looking your loveliest, and is natural looking. Use a double amount of deodorant, since activity does speed up bodily processes. All of which will make you feel better, look better, and thus possibly bowl better.

DEODORANTS   Nothing spoils the illusion of feminine daintiness and, in a sport such as bowling, makes you feel more conspicuous than unsightly perspiration stains.

Therefore a good anti-perspirant and deodorant should be used. And not only under the arms, but this same anti-perspirant should be placed at the bend of the knee and the crook of the arm. There are any number of good anti-perspirant deodorants in roll-on, spray, lotion, or cream form.

FRAGRANCE   A light, delicate cologne is perfect. A dusting of bath powder, followed by a very light misting of cologne over hair and body, would not be overdoing it.

MAKE-UP   A fresh, natural look is what's called for here. What you want is one that is easy to achieve and easy to care for. The best preparation is a light foundation of moisture and emollients that provides a make-up platform and prevents oily shine-through which is a natural outgrowth of exercise. Stimulated bodily processes naturally excrete more oil, tending to make your make-up streaky.

Over the moisture foundation you may prefer a liquid foundation, but I suggest a dusting of cake powder which is an all-in-one make-up that is a combination of foundation and powder. This type doesn't streak or change color on the skin, and is easy to use for touch-ups after you have finished bowling.

Be sure to set your make-up with a square of cotton that has been soaked in cold water and completely wrung out. This sets the foundation so that it will not run.

EYE MAKE-UP   Apply your eye make-up wisely. Use an eyebrow pencil but keep your eye shadow, if you wish to use it, extremely light.

I would also suggest that you use mascara very sparingly. There are roll-on mascaras which are easily applied and which, being waterproof, resist perspiration.

HANDS AND NAILS   Even if your nails are strong, still be sure to reinforce them with extra coats of nail enamel. A sturdy manicure consists of a base coat, two coats of enamel, and a top coat. To this you may add an additional coat of enamel and a top coat. This builds up a shining protective coat of armor.

In filing your nails, use an emery board from side to center. *Be sure to file in one direction.* Your nail is composed of three layers, and when you saw back and forth the friction causes them to separate and peel.

Begin tapering your nail *above the top of your finger.* Never file deeply into the corners or make extreme points. A rounded oval shape with at least one sixteenth of an inch at each side reinforces the nail and gives a more graceful appearance to the finger tips. If your nail is just a stub, file an almost straight-across oval and let the sides grow in.

Soak your hands in warm, soapy water.

Next dampen the end of your orangewood stick, wrap in a wisp of cotton, and dip into cuticle remover. Brush onto the cuticle and under the free edge of the nail. Gently push the cuticle back with the orange-wood stick.

Never press hard as this tends to injure delicate tissue at the cuticle and may cause ridges and marks. Then dry the cuticle with a towel, repeating the gentle pushing-back process with the edge of the towel.

Snip off any stubborn hangnails that remain with nippers or cuticle scissors. *Do not cut the cuticle.* A proper manicure routine eventually will eliminate the need for any cutting.

If your nails are brittle, or tend to peel or crack, you can give them added protection by making slipcovers of a product such as Revlon's Nail Fix.

After your manicure, soak the hands in warm soapsuds and then wipe each nail with cotton dampened in remover to eliminate any trace of oil or moisture, assuring better adhesion of the slipcovers.

After this, make a Nail Fix slipcover for each of your nails in the following manner: Tear off a wedge-shaped piece of Nail Fix tissue the width of each nail at one end and flaring a scant quarter-inch wider at the other. Trim the wide ends into a curve to correspond with each nail tip. Always tear the patch because the ragged edge is less apparent than a clean-cut edge.

You cap the nails one at a time. Start with the little finger of the right hand, if you are right-handed; with the little finger of the left hand if you are left-handed. Because of the added dexterity of your favored hand there is less likelihood of smearing.

Saturate the patch with Nail Fix and lay it flat on the nail with the rounded tip extending approximately one eighth of an inch over the free edge of the nail. Smooth and press the patch to the nail with a finger tip moistened in solvent.

Next turn your hand over so that the palm is uppermost and brush on fresh Nail Fix at the exposed edges of the tissue. Then, with your orangewood stick dipped in solvent, turn the tissue inward over the nail edge, pressing it firmly to the inner surface of the nail. Do this for each finger and allow it to dry thoroughly.

Take a few extra minutes applying these slipcovers and you will find that they not only will last through three or four manicures but also when bowling, will provide added support for your brittle fingernails.

To insure your hands against roughness, when you return from bowling be sure to apply a generous amount of hand lotion.

BOWLING IS NOT NECESSARILY A STRENUOUS SPORT. HOWEVER, IN THE early part of the season a bowler may find a certain amount of stiffness and discomfort in muscles she never knew existed.

Yet even the regular bowler can help to keep her bowling muscles in trim with the special home exercises worked out by Joan Javer, New York regional supervisor for the Vic Tanny gym system of training.

These exercises, which Joan demonstrates on these pages, are designed primarily for the bowler, and yet they will benefit even the non-bowler by putting new elasticity in the thighs and legs, making the back more flexible, tightening the stomach muscles, trimming the hips, loosening the arm and shoulder muscles, firming the pectoral muscles, and generally aiding balance and body control.

THE HEEL TENDON STRETCH   This first exercise is a great aid to balance and body control. It also stretches the heel tendon.

To do this exercise, stand erect, with your feet together. Then with the weight on the left leg take a backward step, starting with the feet about eighteen inches apart from heel to toe. Next bend the front knee as you push down to the floor with the heel of the straight back leg. Return to your erect position. Reverse the legs.

This should help you stretch those tight heel tendons which may be making it difficult for you to go into a full, deep slide when you are bowling.

If you find that your balance and body control are not equal to the task of doing this exercise without support, you can start by doing it as Joan demonstrates in the next set of pictures.

There she stands erect at arm's length from a wall. Then the backward step is taken, a distance of about eighteen inches from heel to toe. Next, keeping the body pushed against the wall with the arms stiffly outstretched, the front knee is bent and the back heel is pushed down until it touches the floor.

The longer the step in this exercise, the better the tendon stretch.

Taking a backward step to start the heel tendon stretch.

Bending the left knee, Joan Javer pushes the right heel down to the floor.

If you lack balance, start the heel tendon stretch with arms outstretched against a wall.

Then take your backward step.

Now, pushing against the wall, bend the front knee and push down with the back leg until the heel touches the floor. The longer the step back, the more tendon stretch.

DEEP-KNEE BEND   This exercise is designed to improve strength and control of the thigh muscles.

Start from the same stance as for the heel tendon stretch, stepping backward with your right foot.

Now bend both knees until the knee of the back leg is even with the heel of the front foot, but do not permit the knee to touch the floor. (See the accompanying picture.)

The arms are outstretched to the side as you lower your body slowly into the kneeling position and then, as you halt your descent with the knee inches from the floor, the body is twisted at the waist so that the arm opposite the front leg is reaching forward and the other stretches out toward the rear. Return the arms to their original position, after this reaching forward, and rise as slowly as possible.

Repeat with the left foot stepping backward.

In the deep-knee bend, take your backward step and then lower the body slowly until the knee is inches from the floor. Now swing the outstretched arms in a full reach forward and backward.

LOWER BACK STRETCH   This is a good exercise for stretching the lower back muscles, but it also will be beneficial for the knees, upper thighs, and the whole back generally.

As you will observe in the pictures, Joan starts from a sitting tuck, raised knees inside the arms, head on knees, and fingers of the extended arms grasping the toes.

Then, keeping her head touching the knees, she slides the heels forward while retaining the hold on the toes. It may be a while before you can extend your legs flat while still keeping your forehead on your knees and retaining a hold on your toes, but you will feel the stretch of your back muscles. Next, you return to the upright position while keeping the forehead on the knees and a firm grip on the toes.

Taking the position for the lower back stretch, knees inside the arms, toes gripped, and head on knees.

Now push out and down on the legs, retaining your grip on your toes and keeping the forehead on the knees.

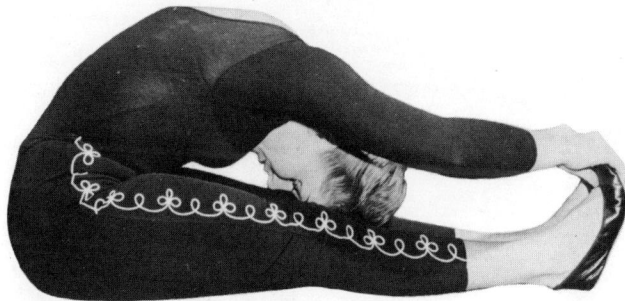

THIGH PULL   Here is another exercise designed to help the lower back
and thigh muscles—and the stomach.

Start from a supine position as Joan demonstrates. Raise the left leg,
grasping the knee with the left hand and the ankle with the right hand.

Then raise the head and the other outstretched leg while pulling the
doubled-up leg to the ear as, simultaneously, you kick straight out with
the extended leg.

This exercise is done on a one-two-three count and, to keep the pull
on the abdomen, change legs while keeping the head and extended leg
off the floor.

Supine position to start the thigh pull.

Raising the left leg, Joan grasps the knee
with the left hand and the ankle with the
right.

Raise the head and extended leg simultaneously, pulling the doubled-up leg to the
ear as you kick out with the extended leg.
Change legs while keeping the head and
legs off the floor.

HIP ROLL   Here we have an exercise that is very good for removing bulges from the hips.

In the accompanying photos you will see that Joan sits erect, with the legs doubled so that the soles of the feet are placed together, her hands grasping the ankles. Next she presses down one knee then the other with the elbow to get a pull on the lower spine.

Then she simply rocks from side to side.

The position for the hip roll, soles together and elbows pushing down on the knees as the hands grip the ankles.

Now rock . . .

And rock!

TUMMY TIGHTENER   This exercise is designed to do just what it says. Joan starts from a supine position, as depicted. Holding the body rigid, she lifts the head until the chin touches the chest as the extended legs are raised three inches off the ground.

At this point the arms are raised and the hands brought together over the body. With head and feet off the floor, the stiff arms then do an up-and-down beat of about six inches, but without touching the body.

Raising the head from the floor first, until it touches the chest, is advocated by Joan for those with a double-chin problem.

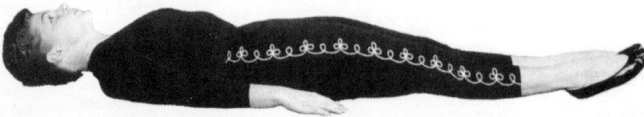

The supine position for starting the tummy tightener.

The head is raised until the chin touches the chest as the extended legs are raised three inches off the floor and the arms are extended rigidly.

The stiff arms do a rapid up-and-down beat without touching the legs.

THE WINDMILL   This exercise will loosen your arm muscles and shoulder joints, and is also good for toning or firming the bust.

Simply stand erect, feet apart, as Joan is demonstrating, and reach
high with the arms. Then, holding the arms rigid and reaching con-
stantly, whirl the hands in small, quick circles.

The windmill, in which your arms are raised
to this position and held rigid as the hands
whirl in small, quick circles.

15 *Bowling in a league*

THE FUN OF BOWLING CAN BECOME MUCH GREATER IF YOU BOWL IN A league. The stimulation of scheduled games and lots of competition will afford you a great deal of pleasure, and also improve your style, because of the systematic practice it involves you in. You get to see lots of players, and that low-score rut hasn't got a chance.

Forming a league is an easy matter. The first steps can be taken through the house you usually bowl in. You can form an open league, with membership consisting of any eligible players, or a closed league, which is one with membership drawn only from the members of a certain group or organization. Many fraternal organizations, church groups, civic organizations, or company organizations have their own bowling teams or leagues.

In order to form a league that will be sanctioned by the American Bowling Congress, you must organize it along the lines approved by the Congress, and obey the playing rules it sets forth.

A league bowls according to a set schedule, and consists of four or more bowling teams or singles leagues. A bowling team is a group of two or more people who have formed a team in order to bowl in a league and/or in tournament competition. A singles league, which must itself apply for regular league sanction, is a group of four or more who are organized to bowl on schedule, and whose standings are based on the results of games played between individual bowlers, rather than on the point system or on total games won or lost by the team itself. The standing of the team, you see, can be determined by any of these methods. The most common method is the four-point system, which gives one point to the winning team of each game, and one point to the team with the highest three-game total pins.

ORGANIZATION OF A LEAGUE   Like most regularized organizations, a league must have a constitution, a set of rules, and officers. The league officers are: president, vice-president, secretary, and treasurer. As is often the case, the secretary and treasurer may be the same person, but each of the other offices must be filled separately. Incidentally, let me suggest that you choose as your secretary-treasurer someone who has the time and ability to keep the league records and weekly averages up to date.

Each team within the league must have a captain, and the captain is responsible for all matters pertaining to the correct conduct of the team, including behavior, promptness at games, and the collection of bowling fees. The fees collected by the captain are remanded to the league secretary.

ABSENTEES   Unless a certain number of eligible players are present to start any game of a series on schedule, the game itself will be forfeited. The basic number of players is called the "legal lineup." If you have a league consisting of five women per team, there must be at least three players present per team. If there are three or four women per team, at least two must be present.

However, members of the forfeiting team are allowed to bowl along with the team winning by forfeit so that their individual scores may be included in the league records. These individuals also are eligible for league or Women's International Bowling Congress awards.

It should be noted here that, if there are not enough players present to compose a legal lineup, blind scores cannot be used.

IF YOU COME LATE   Your league may make special rules to cover cases in which players arrive late to scheduled games. However, even if your rules allow a late player to bowl the entire game, she will still lose her claim for A.B.C. high-score recognition for that game. If your rules don't cover lateness, the late bowler must start her game with the frame her team is bowling when she arrives.

BOWLING ORDER   Your team must bowl in regular order, bowling one frame on one alley and then, for the following frame, bowl in order on the other alley. This is done so that each team bowls five frames in each alley.

Unless she makes a strike, or strikes or spares in the tenth frame, each player shall bowl two balls in every frame. The only pins which will actually score are those the player knocks down. None will be conceded. If, in the tenth frame, a player makes a strike, she may roll two more balls in the same lane. If a player bowls a spare in the tenth frame, she will be allowed one more ball.

WHO BOWLS FIRST   There may come a time when the outcome of the game, and even that of the series, depends on how the last bowler of each team does in the final frame. Now comes the question as to who has to shoot first. The answer is that the bowler on the right has to roll first. Even if her pins aren't set up, the anchor woman on the left alley, if she chooses, may wait until the pins are set and her opponent bowls.

IN CASE OF A TIE   When a game ends in a tie, each team will record half a game won and half a game lost. If the point system is used, each team will be credited with one half the value of the point or points involved.

WINNING BY FORFEIT   Even if the rival team does not show up and your team wins by forfeit, your team must bowl its scheduled games just as if you had competition. Every frame must be completed on one alley before the team starts the next frame on the adjoining alley.

DECIDING ON YOUR LINEUP   There is a definite strategy in setting your lineup. Your lead-off bowler should be the pepper-pot type who is a consistent spare shooter. Her enthusiasm and example will do much to put the team in a mood where "everybody marks."

Placing your lowest-average bowler in the middle of the lineup will do much to take the pressure off her. Then you should have your two highest-average bowlers in the final positions. Your last bowler, or "anchor," should be your most reliable player, for often it may be up to her to mark in the last frame and pull a close one out of the fire.

KINDS OF LEAGUES   Leagues fall into three categories: open, handicap, and classified.

In the open, or "scratch," league, the outcome of the game depends on the scores themselves.

In the handicap league, a handicap is set for each player. This handicap is determined by the difference between a "scratch" average and the player's own average. If the scratch average is 150, then the player's handicap is the difference between 150 and her own average.

A classified league is one in which the team's over-all average determines its entry into the league. If a team averages over a specified figure, say 800, it may not enter the league specifying that average as its limit.

16 *The bowling rules you should know*

(*Courtesy Women's International Bowling Congress*)

PLAYING RULES COVERING EVERY SITUATION IN BOWLING ARE AVAILABLE, and a complete set may be obtained from the Women's International Bowling Congress.

The following, taken from the official rule book, are those that affect the average bowler and which she should know.

LEGAL PINFALL   Every ball delivered by the player shall count, unless declared a dead ball. Pins must then be respotted after the cause for declaring such a dead ball has been removed.

(A) Pins that are knocked down by another pin or pins rebounding in play from the side partition or rear cushion are counted as pins down.

(B) If when rolling at a full setup or in order to make a spare, it is discovered immediately after the ball has been delivered that one or more pins are improperly set, although not missing, the ball and resulting pinfall shall be counted. It is each player's responsibility to determine if the setup is correct. She shall insist that any pins incorrectly set be respotted before delivering her ball, for otherwise she implies that the setup is satisfactory. No change in the position of any pins left standing can be made after a previous delivery in order to make a spare, unless the pin setter has moved or misplaced any pin after the previous delivery and prior to the bowling of the next ball.

(C) Pins that are knocked down by a fair ball and remain lying on the alley bed or in the gutters, or which lean so as to touch kickbacks or side partitions, are termed dead wood and counted as pins down, and must be removed before the next ball is bowled.

ILLEGAL PINFALL   When any of the following incidents occurs the ball counts as a ball rolled, but pins knocked down shall not count:

(1) When pins are knocked down or displaced by a ball that leaves the lane before reaching the pins.

(2) When a ball rebounds from the rear cushion.

(3) When pins come in contact with the body, arms, or legs of a pin setter and rebound.

(4) A standing pin that falls upon removal of dead wood or is knocked down by a pin setter or mechanical pin-setting equipment shall not count, and must be replaced on the pin spot inscribed on the pin deck where it originally stood before delivery of the ball.

(5) Pins that are bowled off the alley bed, rebound, and remain standing on the alley bed must be counted as pins standing.

(6) If in delivering the ball a foul is committed, any pins knocked down by such delivery shall not be counted.

DEAD BALL   A ball shall be declared dead if any of the following circumstances occurs, in which case such ball shall not count. The pins must be respotted after the cause for declaring such dead ball has been removed, and player shall be required to rebowl.

(A) If after the player delivers her ball attention is immediately called to the fact that one or more pins were missing from the setup.

(B) When a pin spotter removes or interferes with any pin or pins before they stop rolling or before the ball reaches the pins.

(C) When a player bowls on the wrong lane or out of turn.

(D) When the player is interfered with by a pin setter, another bowler, a spectator, or a moving object as the ball is being delivered and before delivery is completed, she must then and there accept the resulting pinfall or demand that pins be respotted.

(E) When any pins at which she is bowling are moved or knocked down in any manner as she is delivering the ball and before the ball reaches the pins.

(F) When a player's ball comes in contact with any foreign obstacle.

NO PINS MAY BE CONCEDED   No pins may be conceded and only those actually knocked down or moved entirely off the playing surface of the bowling lane as a result of the legal delivery of the ball by the player may be counted. Every frame must be completed at the time the player is bowling in her regular order.

REPLACEMENT OF PINS   A broken pin does not change the score made by a bowler. The number of pins knocked down are counted, after which the broken pin is replaced.

BOWLING ON WRONG LANE   Should a team start a game on the wrong lane and the error is discovered prior to the start of the second frame, the game must be started over on the lane on which the team was scheduled.

   If the error is not discovered until other frames than the first have been bowled, the team shall bowl two frames in succession on the lane on which the team was scheduled to start, thereafter alternating on each lane until the game is completed, thus ending on the correctly scheduled lane.

   A team starting a game on the correct lane and then bowling one frame or more on the wrong lane shall bowl two frames in succession on the lane on which the team failed to bowl, thus ending the game on the correctly scheduled lane.

FOULS   A foul is committed, with no pinfall credited to the player although the ball counts as a ball rolled, when a part of the bowler's person encroaches upon or goes beyond the foul line and touches any part of the lane equipment or building, during or after executing a legal delivery. A ball is in play and a foul may be called after legal delivery has been made and until the same or another player is on the approach in position to make a succeeding delivery.

   If the player commits a foul apparent to both captains or one or more members of each of the opposing teams competing in a league or tournament on the same pair of lanes where the foul is committed, or to the official scorer or tournament official, and should the foul umpire or judge through negligence fail to see it committed or an approved auto-

It's a foul when you slide across the foul line as Carol Christensen is doing here. The pins you get don't count and are respotted.

Touching any part of the building beyond the foul line, as I am demonstrating here, also is a foul.

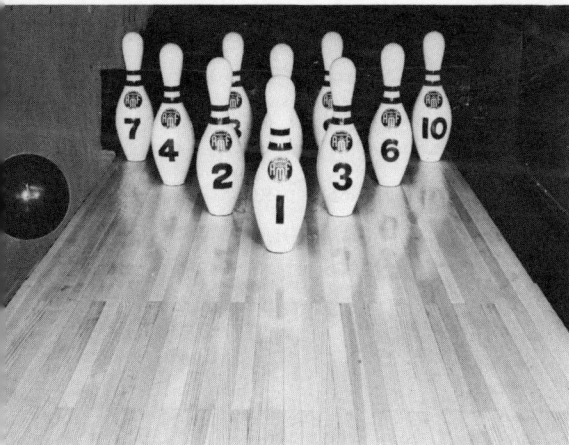

If your ball is in the gutter, as depicted here, and bounces out to knock down some pins, they do not count.

matic foul device fail to record it, a foul shall nevertheless be declared and so recorded.

FOUL COUNTS AS BALL BOWLED A foul ball shall be recorded as a ball bowled by the player, but any pins bowled down when a foul is committed shall not count.

When the player fouls upon delivering the first ball of a frame, all pins knocked down must be respotted, and only those pins knocked down by the second ball may be counted. If she bowls down all the pins with her second ball after fouling with the first, it shall be scored as a spare. When less than ten pins are bowled down on the second ball after fouling on the first, it shall be scored as an error.

A player who fouls when delivering the second ball of a frame shall be credited with only those pins bowled down with her first ball, provided no foul was committed when the first ball was delivered. When the bowler fouls during the delivery of her first ball in the tenth frame and bowls down all ten pins with her second ball (making a spare), she bowls a third ball and is credited with a spare plus the pins bowled down with the third ball. When a player fouls while delivering her third ball in the tenth frame, only those pins bowled down in delivering her first two balls shall be counted.

AVERAGES A bowling average is determined by dividing the total number of pins credited to a bowler by the number of games bowled in one league in a season.

Composite Average: The average of all leagues when a player bowls in two or more leagues. This average is determined by adding the total pins for all leagues and dividing the results by the total number of games bowled in all leagues.

Highest Average: The best average in one of several leagues in which a player competes.

In all cases, extra pins or fractions must be disregarded when using averages for handicapping or classification purposes. The extra pins shall be reduced to a percentage of a pin only for the purpose of deciding individual position standings in a league.

RUNWAYS   No one shall mark or introduce on any part of the approach or lane any substance which will have a tendency to injure, disfigure, or place the runway or lane in such a condition as to detract from the possibility of other bowlers being able to take advantage of the usual conditions.

The use of such substances as aristol, talcum powder, pumice, resin, and so forth, on shoes, and the use of soft rubber soles and heels that rub off and in any manner alter the normal condition of the runway, are strictly prohibited.

17 *Language of the lanes*

(*Courtesy American Bowling Congress*)

A

Anchor: Last woman in the team lineup.
Apple: The ball.

"Apple"

Arch: To increase the width of your hook.

B

Baby split: The 2-7 or 3-10 splits.
Backup: Ball that curves from left to right.
Backup alley: An alley that holds or tends to prevent a ball from rolling to the right.
Barmaid: A hidden pin.
Bed: The alley bed.
Bedposts: The 7-10 split.

"Bedposts"

Belly the ball: To arch or increase the width of your hook from an inside- or middle-lane starting point.

Bench work: Conversation intended to upset or disconcert opponents.

Big ball: Hook that enables the bowler to hit almost any place for strikes.

Big ears: The 4-6-7-10 split.

Big fill: Anything over 8 on a spare.

Big five: Three pins on one side and two on the other as, for instance, the 4-7 on the left and the 6-9-10 on the right.

Big four: The 4-6-7-10 split.

Blind: Score given a team for an absent member.

Blow: An error. Failing to spare, except in the case of a split.

Board: Boards composing the alley bed.

Body English: Body gyrations wishfully intended to steer the ball after its release.

Bolsa: Western term for a thin hit, or one light of the head pin.

Box: Synonym of frame.

Bridge: Distance between finger holes.

Brooklyn: Ball crossing over to strike the left of the head pin.

Broom ball: Wide hook that seems to sweep the pins off the lane.

Bucket: The 2-4-5-8 for the right-hander, or the 3-5-6-9 for the left-hander. *Also* "dinner bucket."

C

CC: 200 game.

Cheese cakes: Lanes where strikes are easy to get.

Cherry: Ball that chops off the front pin of a spare and leaves the pin behind and/or to the right or left standing. It is an error, blow, or miss.

Chinamen: In some sections, those pins directly behind others, such as the 5-8-9; in other sections the "Chinaman" is the 1-2-4-10 setup.

Choke: To become overanxious and hence fail to make a shot.

Chop: Picking a cherry; a pick.

"Christmas Tree"

Christmas tree: The 3-7-10 for a right-hander; 2-7-10 for the left-hander.

Cincinnati: The 8-10 split.

Count: The number of pins knocked down on your first ball to be used in the previous frame for computing your spare score.

Creeper: A slow ball.

Crooked arm: Type of hook-ball bowler who bends his elbow. In some localities, all hook bowlers are called "crooked arms."

Cross alley: To aim to the left from the extreme right-hand corner of the approach, or to the right from the extreme left-hand corner.

Cross-over: The ball going to the left of the head pin. Also a Brooklyn or a Jersey.

Crow hopper: A clawlike, loose grip on ball, noticeable just at the release over the foul line.

Curtain: Anchor woman "blowing" in tenth frame when a spare would have won for her team.

Curve: A ball that works to the left from the moment it contacts the lane. Some bowlers call it a "hook," but a hook ball waits until it nears the pins before it breaks to the left.

Cushion: Upholstered back section of the pit.

Cutter: A sharp-breaking hook that cuts down the pins.

D

Dead apple: Ball that fades or deflects easily when it hits the pins; ineffective ball.

Dead ball: An ineffective ball.

Deflection: Action of the pins on the ball when it hits them, causing the ball to veer and change direction.

Dime store: The 5-10 split.

Dinner bucket: Same as "bucket."

Dinner pail: Same as "bucket" and "dinner bucket."

Dive: An alley on which your ball takes a last-minute big hook or dive to the left.

Dodo: Head pin with the 10 pin up. Obsolete.

Double: Two strikes in succession.

Double balling: Throwing a second ball before the first is returned. (Bad bowling manners.)

Double pinochle: The 4-6-7-10 split.

"Double Pinochle"

Double pinochle with the ace of spades: The 4-6-7-10 split plus the 9 pin.

Double wood: One pin directly behind another.

Drive: Synonym for lane.

Dummy: Score decided upon by the league to use for an absentee.

Dutch 200: A 200 game made by alternate strikes and spares.

Dutchman: Same as the "Dutch 200."

E

Eight-ten: The 8-10 split.

Error: A miss.

F

Faith, Hope, and Charity: The 3-7-10 Christmas Tree or the 2-7-10 for left-handers.

Fast: In this book "fast" describes a lane that is highly polished and consequently holds down the hook. Some authorities feel it is more accurate to speak of lanes as either "holding" or "running."

Fence posts: The 7-10 split.

Fill: The number of pins knocked down following a spare.

Flat alley: A neutral lane, or one that does not run or hold. The term is applied to the lane's action, not its levelness.

Flat arc: Technical term describing the curve of a ball in process of delivery. Some bowlers allow their ball to describe a perfect arc or a part of a circle. Others keep the ball low to the runway and this "flat arc" is not a true circle.

Floater: A ball that goes where the lane lets it; not a hook or backup insofar as its axis of rotation is concerned.

Foul: Touching or going beyond the foul line as you deliver the ball.

Foul line: The line that determines the beginning of the lane.

Foundation: A strike in the ninth frame.

Four-six: The 4-6 split.

Four-timer: Getting four strikes in a row.

Frame: One-tenth part of a game. The squares on a score sheet indicating each tenth of the game are called frames or boxes.

Full hit: When the ball strikes near the center of the head pin or any pin at which you may be shooting.

G

Getting the wood: Knocking down a good score; forestry, woodpile, lumber, timber.

Go the route: To finish the game with three or more consecutive strikes.

Golden gate: The 4-6-7-10 or big four split.

Grab: The ball dives or takes a hook suddenly.

Grasshopper: A good working ball that splashes the pins.
Graveyards: Tough lanes. Usually the tougher pair in an establishment.
Groove: An apparent depression that carries the ball into the pocket.
Gutter ball: A ball that goes into the gutter.

H

Hard way: Getting 200 by alternate strikes and spares; same as the "Dutch 200."
Head pin: The Number 1 pin.

"Head Pin"

High board: A much misused expression to describe two conditions on an alley bed. Owing to atmospheric conditions one board in a bed may contract or expand a trifle. If a ball rolls over this place, its course is changed. Most boards contract and leave a low spot, yet this condition is spoken of as a "high board."
High hit: A hit where the ball strikes a pin near the center.
High 10 and 30: Western term for high game and high three-game total. Also, "High 50 and 150" means high team game and total. This refers to frames in a game or series.
Higher: Refers to degree of fullness of a previous hit and means to have the ball slightly more to the left.
Hit 'em right: A catcall used when a ball fails to carry one pin on a good hit.
Hold: The action of a lane to resist hook action.
Holding alley: A lane that resists hook action.
Hole: The 1-3 pocket.
Home lane: Several meanings. If a bowler gets several strikes on one lane and none on the other, he speaks of the former as his "home lane." Teams that favor one pair in a house call them their "home lanes." Also refers to the establishment where a traveling team rolls all its games.
Honey: A good ball.
Hook: A ball that breaks sharply to the left.
Hook alley: A lane on which the ball is inclined to break to the left.
Hot: A bowler gets hot when he starts stringing strikes.

I

"In there": Ball was a good pocket hit.

Inside stuff: Same as "bench work."

J

Jack Manders: Goes through the middle of a 7-10 split, or any wide one.

Jersey side: To the left of the head pin; same as a "Brooklyn."

"Jersey Side"

K

Kegeler-kegel: A synonym for bowlers, coming from the German word *Kegel*. Americanized way of spelling is kegler, kegling; but many prefer kegeler or kegeling.

Kickback: The division boards between lanes at the pit end.

Kick-off: Effective delivery of a good ball.

Kindling wood: Light pins.

King pin: The head pin; in some sections the 5 pin.

Kitty: The money collected by team captain from members for errors, splits, and other prearranged fines; usually divided equally or to be used to defray expenses to tournaments or for post-season affairs.

Kresge: In sections where the 5-10 split is called the "Woolworth," the 5-7 is spoken of as the "Kresge."

L

Lane: Synonym for alley.

Late ten: Strike in which the 10 pin is the last to be knocked down. Similarly, "late four."

Lead off: First woman in a team's lineup.

Leave: Pins remaining after the first ball is thrown.

Lift: Giving the ball an upward motion with the fingers at point of release.

"Light"

Light: Hit not "full" enough; also called "thin."

Lights out: When the anchor woman blows spare in the tenth frame which would have won the game for her team; same as "curtains."

Lily: The impossible 5-7-10 split.

Loaf: Not putting proper hook action on the ball so that it fails to come up to the objective.

Lofting: Throwing the ball out on the lane too far beyond the foul line.

Looper: A hook ball that describes a wide arc. Bowlers usually describe an "out and in" ball as a looper.

Loose hit: The ball hits the head-pin thin, creating unusually devastating action off the kickback.

Low hit: A ball is low if it hits the head pin thin; opposed to "high" or "full."

M

Make it fit: Trying to make the 4-5, 9-10, or types of splits where both sides of the ball must contact the pins.

Maples: Synonym for the pins.

Mark: To get a strike or spare.

Miss: An error or blow.

Mother-in-law: The Number 7 pin.

Move around: To change the starting position in order to adjust for lane conditions.

Move in: To start from or near a center position on the runway.

Move out: To start from or near a corner position on the runway.

Mule ears: The 7-10 split; same as "bedposts."

Murphy: The baby split.

N

Nose hit: A hit full on the head pin.

"Nose Hit"

O

One in the dark: The rear pin in the 1-5, 2-8, or 3-9 combinations.

Open frame: A frame without a strike or a spare.

Out and in: A wide hook on a running lane where the bowler sets his ball in the center and aims it toward the gutter. The hook comes back to the head pin; hence "out and in."

Outside: Refers to playing certain lanes more or less toward the corner position, as compared to being in the center of the runway.

P

Part of the building: Expression used when the 7 or 10 pin stands on a good hit.

Perfect strike: A ball that hits evenly the pocket between the 1 and 3 pins.

Pick: Chopping off some pins but leaving others standing when shooting a spare.

"Pick"

Picket fence: The 1-2-4-7 or 1-3-6-10.

Pinching the ball: Gripping the ball too hard and thus causing an unnatural delivery.

Pit: Space to the rear of the lane, into which the pins are hit.

Pitch: The angle at which the bowling ball hole is bored.

Pocket: The 1-3 "hole" for the right-hander; the 1-2 for the left-hander.

Point: To aim higher at the head pin. A variant of "push 'em up."

Poison ivy: The 3-6-10 setup.

Poodle: To roll the ball in the gutter.

Powder puff: A slow ball that fails to carry; same as "puff ball."

Powerhouse: A strike ball that carries all ten pins into the pit.

Puddle: A gutter ball.

Puff ball: A slow ball that fails to carry; same as "powder puff."

Pumpkin: Synonym for bowling ball.

Push 'em up: Push the ball from a corner position toward the head pin.

R

Rail: Slang for "railroad."

Railroad: Synonym for split.

Rat club: A team that shoots unusually low scores for one game.

Return: The track on which balls roll from the pit to the ball rack.

Reverse: A severe backup.

Run: A lane runs if it takes a hook.

Running alley: A lane that takes a hook. Opposed to "holding lane."

Runway: The approach or platform on which the bowler stands and delivers the ball.

S

Sandwich game: Same as "Dutch 200."

Schleifer: A thin hit strike, similar to the spiller type. Usually applied to a thin Brooklyn hit where the pins seem to fall one by one.

Scratch: To use actual scores.

Short pin: A pin that is rolling on the lane and fails to hit a standing pin.

Skidding-sliding: An improperly turned ball. Also refers to action on newly refinished lanes.

Sleeper: A hidden pin.

"Sleeper"

Slot lane: A lane where strikes are easy to get.

Slow lane: A double-meaning word. Some call a "slow lane" one in which the ball holds; others one on which they get a bigger hook. In this book, it's one where the ball takes more quickly and gives you the bigger hook.

Small ball: A ball that has to hit the pocket almost perfectly for strikes.

Snake eyes: The 7-10 split.

Snow plow: A wide hook that sweeps the pins off the lane; same as a "sweeper."

Soft alley: A lane where strikes are easy to get.

Sour apple: A poor ball, one that fades to leave up the 5-7 or 5-10.

Southpaw: A left-hander.

Span: Distance between thumb and finger hole.

Spare: All pins knocked down on two balls.

Spiller: A different type of strike from a thin hit, where the pins seem to melt away. This strike takes longer to develop than the other types.

Splash: A strike where the pins are knocked off almost instantaneously.

Split: Combinations of pins left standing after the first delivery in a frame, with a pin down immediately ahead of or between them.

Spot: A place on the lane at which a bowler is aiming.

Squeeze: Gripping the ball too hard; same as "pinching."

Steal: To get more pins than deserved on a hit.

Stiff alley: A holding lane; a fast lane that resists a hook.

Strike: All pins knocked down on the first ball.

Striking out: Striking to the finish of the game.

Sweeper: A wide hook that seems to sweep the pins off the alley.

T

Tandem: Two pins, one behind the other, such as the 1-5, the 2-8, and the 3-9.

Tap: A pin is left standing on an apparently perfect hit.

Telephone poles: Heavy pins. In some sections, the 7-10 split.

Thin: A hit where the ball barely touches the head pin.

Three-quarters: The spot midway between the corner and the center of the lane and three-quarters of the width of the lane from the left corner where bowler places his ball.

Throwing rocks: Throwing a lot of good strike balls.

Turkey: Three strikes in a row.

U

Umbrella ball: A nose hit that results in a strike.

Up the hill: A coaxing expression used to get a delivered ball into the pocket.

W

Washout: The 1-2-10 or the 1-2-4-10 spare.

Win all but three: The explanation of a team that has lost three games in league play.

Winding them in: A hook bowler hitting the pocket consistently.

Wooden bottles: Pins.

Woolworth: The 5-10 split.

Working ball: A ball with great spin that produces a lot of action among the pins.